To the greatest
gal
at

Betty Oliger Fox
AKA The
Foxy
Lady!

THE PRIVILEGE OF MAN IS TO DREAM

Mark Twain's Visit to Hawaii

Bettye Oliger Fox

All rights reserved. No part of this book shall be reproduced or transmitted in any form or by any means, electronic, mechanical, magnetic, photographic including photocopying, recording or by any information storage and retrieval system, without prior written permission of the publisher. No patent liability is assumed with respect to the use of the information contained herein. Although every precaution has been taken in the preparation of this book, the publisher and author assume no responsibility for errors or omissions. Neither is any liability assumed for damages resulting from the use of the information contained herein.

Copyright © 2013 by Bettye Oliger Fox

ISBN 978-0-7414-8459-8 Paperback
ISBN 978-0-7414-8460-4 eBook
Library of Congress Control Number: 2013906241

Printed in the United States of America

Published May 2013

INFINITY PUBLISHING
1094 New DeHaven Street, Suite 100
West Conshohocken, PA 19428-2713
Toll-free (877) BUY BOOK
Local Phone (610) 941-9999
Fax (610) 941-9959
Info@buybooksontheweb.com
www.buybooksontheweb.com

Dedicated to my mother, Audree Velma Stobaugh Oliger
My daughter, Scarlet Katherine Andrews
My mentor at Texas Woman's University, Dr. Phyllis Bridges

Mark Twain's Prose Poem about Hawaii

No alien land in all the world has any deep, strong charm for me but that one, no other land could so longingly and so beseechingly haunt me sleeping and waking, through half a lifetime, as that one has done. Other things leave me, but it abides; other things change, but it remains the same. For me its balmy airs are always blowing, its summer seas flashing in the sun, the pulsing of its surf-beat is in my ear; I can see its garlanded crags, its leaping cascades, its plumy palms drowsing by the shore, its remote summits floating like islands above the cloud rack; I can feel the spirit of its woodland solitudes. I can hear the splash of its brooks; in my nostrils still lives the breath of flowers that perished twenty years ago. (qtd. in Frear 217)

CHAPTER ONE

"O ke kanaka ke kuleana o ka moe"
(The privilege of man is to dream)

Within the human imagination a strange current flows deeply; ancient legends speak of the romantic lure of the islands, warm waters, cool breezes of trade winds, a tropical paradise that offers one an escape from daily cares and an opportunity for the fulfillment of dreams.

The future American novelist, Mark Twain, sought the romantic lure of the Hawaiian Islands in March, 1866. In the Sandwich Islands Mark Twain first discovered beauty. It should be added that in the Sandwich Islands he also discovered the dream. "His first passages embodying the dream as his expression of beauty were written in the Sandwich Islands" (Bellamy 219).

The fantasy aspects of beauty as the dream, the picture, and the magic fairy world of the Islands were to color and shade Mark Twain's vision of life. "His preoccupation with the dream motif is a manifestation of that part of his complex personality which was essentially escapist" (Bellamy 219). Years later Mark Twain would reflect back to his memorable 1866 visit:

I visited, a great many years ago, the Sandwich Islands--that peaceful land, that beautiful land, that far off home of profound repose, and soft indolence, and dreamy solitude, where life is one long slumberous Sabbath, the climate one long delicious summer day, and the good that die experience no change, for they but fall asleep in one heaven and wake up in another. (qtd. in M. Clemens, *The Honolulu Star-Bulletin 7* Dec)

Samuel Langhorne Clemens (1835-1910) was a young man of thirty when he boarded the sail-steamer *Ajax* on March 7, 1866, to venture on an ocean voyage to the Hawaiian Islands. He did not have a great knowledge of life, but he did have a high estimation for life and the adventures that no doubt would be waiting ahead.

The Privilege of Man is to Dream

In 1866 Mark Twain's *nom de plume* was recent, and had been seldom set in type.

"He had seen much of America, an America that was to become immortal through his pages. His adventures had been rich in human experience, but he had as yet made no especial mark as a writer" (Vandercook xi).

Mark Twain had not yet married when he visited the Sandwich Islands. He had not yet written *Huckleberry Finn*, *Tom Sawyer*, and *Life on the Mississippi*; nor had he lectured. He was poor and not yet internationally known. Earlier that year, during a low period, he put a pistol to his head but did not succeed. During this same low period in February 1866, an editor on the *Gold Hill News* (Nevada) described him in print as a "Bohemian from the sagebrush, a jailbird, bail-jumper, deadbeat, and alcoholic who had probably contacted a venereal disease from rolls in a whorehouse" (Kaplan 62). Clemens's answer was to depart in silence, as correspondent at twenty dollars for each weekly dispatch for *The Sacramento Union*, the most powerful paper in the West. He was sent to "ransack the Islands, the cataracts and volcanoes completely, and write 20-30 letters" (Pitchford 35).

In the four months Mark Twain spent in Hawaii as a roving reporter for *The Sacramento Union*, he went on his first excursion outside the United States, an appointment with his dreams that embarked him in the next few years on a new and lucrative profession--public speaking.

Mark Twain was a public speaker before he became a literary man. He was one of the most sought-after public speakers of his day, commanding the highest prices ever paid to a speaker. He appeared on the rostrum for the first time on October 2, 1866, in San Francisco, speaking about his recent trip to Hawaii (Shavelenko 145). The newspapers gave him good reviews. As one reporter put it: "Mark Twain has put the tiny, remote monarchy on the map-and in fair exchange, the islands have put Mark Twain on the map, too-- the map of literary America" (Pitchford 36).

The majority of American readers know the Mark Twain of humor, white suits and the Mississippi River, but how many people know that the single most important turning point in the career of Samuel Langhorne Clemens came because of Hawaii..." (Horton 88). Walter Francis Frear agrees with Horton:

> The visit marked the most significant turning point of Mark Twain's life, the interstice between the thirty years of preparation in the extraordinary rough school of his early experience and the forty-five years of his phenomenal career as writer, lecturer, and personality. The trip was an oasis in his life as refreshing as a golden memory and marked the transition from his earlier crude writings, as well as giving him a new and sorely needed, lucrative profession--lecturer. (Frear viii)

Douglas Grant also agrees that writing *The Letters* was a turning point because Twain later was able to use portions of them in *Roughing It* (1872), foreshadowing exactly the book in which he was to make his name and a fortune--*The Innocents Abroad* (Grant 31).

For the next year and a half the Sandwich Islands lectures were Mark Twain's sole source of income. Throughout his lecture career the subject of the Sandwich Islands was "his surest bet to insure a successful platform evening" (Pitchford 36). What started out to be a different and desperate attempt to make a living for Samuel Clemens "carried him through 40 years of lecture and reading engagements ... doing much to add to Mark Twain's immortality" (Pitchford 36). With this speaking career came another of traveling correspondent, producing *The Innocents Abroad,* and world-wide fame as an author in two years.

For the first time in his writing career, Mark Twain glimpsed scenes of a Pacific land unfamiliar to him and his reading audience. "The necessity of complete communication, the realization that none of the background could be taken for granted, put the special correspondent on his mettle" (Ferguson 107). Lewis Leary also agrees: "These Sandwich Islands letters set to form the pattern which four years later was to establish Mark Twain's reputation with *Innocents Abroad*" (Leary 16).

Mark Twain himself believed that there are numerous turning points in a person's life, each a link in a long chain and each link seeming more crucial that its predecessor. Recounting the links, or turning points, that led to his career as a journalist, he came to one that led him from a journalist's occupation to the higher calling of a literary career. That link was forged by circumstances which had sent him to the Sandwich Islands.

From the communication stimulus of these circumstances must be "ascribed the literary superiority of the Sandwich Islands letters over any of his previous work" (Ferguson 107). The *Ajax* trip was pivotal, for it provided Mark Twain with an opportunity for sustained writing. "The assignment combined both travel and observation, a combination that was to prove fruitful both in travel books and in novels" (Emerson 31).

Mark Twain was weary of working as a struggling writer in Nevada and California, and had only attracted some attention with "The Jumping Frog." It was in high spirits that Mark Twain left San Francisco that March. Although he had only planned to spend one month in the islands, he spent four months there. "They were probably the happiest months of his adult life" (Gerber 19).

Taylor agrees and quotes Mark Twain:

> I was in the islands to write letters for the weekly edition of the *Sacramento Union*, a rich and influential daily journal which hadn't any use for them, but could afford to spend twenty dollars a week for nothing. I dearly wanted to see the islands, and they listened to me and gave me the opportunity. (qtd. in Taylor 12)

Mark Twain's twenty-five picturesque letters he wrote as a roving reporter for the *Sacramento Union*, printed in both daily and weekly editions, provided him an exposure opportunity he had not had before. "Sam Clemens, the itinerant journalist, became Mark Twain the writer" (Vandercook xi).

To appreciate what the name Mark Twain meant before Hawaii, consider that his first letter from the Sandwich Islands appeared in the *Union* with only this editorial preface: "We publish letters from special correspondents at Boston, New York, Washington and Honolulu" (Horton 92). Twain's letter ran last.

Steamship service between San Francisco and Honolulu had just been established, and a sizable interest in the Sandwich Islands (later the Hawaiian Islands) as a place for travel and commercial investment was fast developing (Gerber 19). Some letters covered sugar and whaling industries, which were of interest to American businessmen at that time, and also the Hawaiian trade, "whose exports brought high fees to the United States Customs" (Day, *Mark Twain's Letters* vii). The year 1866 was a quiet year in the Hawaiian Islands. The whaling trade was in decline, and sugar was not the primary industry yet. Steam engines had brought the Islands closer to the United States and "caused considerable speculation about the future of tourism" (Abramson, *Letters* 1).

Not only did Mark Twain give the outside world a social view of these remote areas of the Pacific Ocean, he commented on political areas as well. A. Grove Day recommends a close reading of these Sandwich Islands letters to anyone who wishes a frank and sometimes violent view of Hawaii in the reign of the fifth Kamehameha (Day, *Mark Twain's Letters* viii). Although an independent monarchy still existed in Hawaii in 1866, the day of foreign influence was at hand. Citizens in the United States were interested in several aspects about the islands. The native population of Hawaii was in decline, and in the year 1866 a period of calm was soon to erupt at the edge of boom and Americanization (Abramson, *Letters* 2).

Mark Twain took his assignment seriously. Through the nineteen days of the voyage to Honolulu, except when he came down with the mumps, he jotted in his travel notebooks all types of information about the Islands from returning travelers. Many passengers developed seasickness, and Twain extracted from these vomitings crude humor to write about in his first letters to the *Union*.

Mark Twain carried with him, for purposes of comic relief, his fictitious friend and imaginary traveling companion, Mr. Brown (of the Q.C. Snodgrass letters), who had first appeared in a Californian sketch as early as March 18, 1865. Brown became an inseparable part of Mark Twain's writings from 1865 until the *Innocents Abroad*. Brown runs through not only this first series of travel letters but the future travel letters as well. He was likened to Sancho Panza and Mephistopheles and suggests other literary characters as well. "He has been characterized as vulgarian, realist, philosopher, skeptic, cynic, pessimist, alter ego, inner voice, irreverent, irrepressible" (Frear 99). "The more vulgar utterances about smells, seasickness and insects, were, from the beginning of the Sandwich Islands letters, all attributed to Brown, instead of being spoken by Mark himself" (Ferguson 107). Mr. Brown's sweetheart, Twain boasted, was "so elegant that she picked her nose with a fork. When passengers became seasick Brown was thoughtful, passing from one to the other saying it was all right" (Leary 16).

Frear believes that Mr. Brown had two principal functions for Mark Twain. First, Brown enabled Twain to put forth the voice and mind of another the things he thought should not be held back and felt it was not quite proper to say himself. The second purpose for Brown was that he served as a kind of butt or subject of humor, especially the cruder kind (Frear 100). Brown arrived in Honolulu with Twain.

The Honolulu Commercial Advertiser noted the arrival on the *Ajax* of a Miss Nellie Freeman, a celebrated vocalist who would appear at the local theater. The same paper carried an advertisement that celebrated the arrival of the *Ajax*, but Twain's name was noted in the local press only in the list of *Ajax* passengers--in small print (Abramson, *Letters* 3).

As the first reporter from America to cover the Hawaiian Islands in the period of time after the Civil War, Mark Twain disembarked the steamship *Ajax* on Sunday morning, March 18, 1866. It was not until mid-May that Honolulu newspapers made much note of Twain's arrival. By then his letters had begun appearing in *The Sacramento Union*, and some of his earlier letters had made their way back to Honolulu:

> This humorous correspondent of the *Sacramento Union*, whose first letters from Honolulu appear in that paper of April 21st, is now making a tour of the islands. His real name is Samuel Clemens, but he is better known under his

nom de plume given above ... his letters abound in good humor and fun, though if he would stick a little closer to facts, they would be more reliable. (Abramson, *Letters* 3)

Most important of the letters in enabling him to achieve fame was the 15th, in which Twain reported his scoop on the burning at sea of the clipper ship *Hornet* May 3, 1866, and the remarkable survival of its captain, 12 crew members, and two passengers after drifting in the Pacific Ocean in an open longboat before reaching land on June 15, 1866, at Laupahoehoe on the Big Island of Hawaii. It was a brilliant piece of reporting.

What had caused the fire? The following was reported by Mark Twain:

> At seven o'clock on the morning of the 3rd of May, the chief mate and two men started down into the hold to draw some bright varnish from a cask. The captain told them to bring the cask on deck—that it was dangerous to have it where it was, in the hold. The mate, instead of obeying the order, proceeded to draw a can full of the varnish first. He had an open light in his hand, and the liquid took fire; the can was dropped, the officer in his consternation neglected to close the bung, and in a few seconds the fiery torrent had run in every direction, under bales of rope, cases of candles, barrels of kerosene, and all sorts of freight, and tongues of flame were shooting upward through every aperture and crevice toward the deck ... and the cabin was a hell of angry flames

... the lifeboats were launched, and a month and a half of slow drifting lay ahead of the crew. (Branch 172)

When the *Hornet* survivors first arrived in Honolulu, Twain was in bed suffering from backside saddle boils received from a horseback trip he had taken around the Big Island. His friend, Anson Burlingame, American Ambassador to China, had him carried on a stretcher from his lodgings to where the starved survivors were recuperating. As Mark Twain says: "Anson Burlingame came and put me on a stretcher and had me carried to the hospital where the shipwrecked men were, and I never needed to ask a question. He attended to all of that himself, and I had nothing to do but make the notes" (Taylor P of P 13).

The survivors had suffered in an open boat for forty-three days experiencing hunger, delirium, exposure, and the threat of cannibalism. It was a journalist's dream scoop. While Burlingame conducted the interview, Twain made notes, got hold of the dairies of the Captain, and returned home to work furiously on the story through the night (Vandercook xiii). Captain Josian Mitchell recorded in his diary that not a man could walk (Taylor P of P 12).

Mark Twain tried to play down the thoughts of cannibalism that drifted through the men's minds while adrift, and he brilliantly recorded the hardships endured by the men. He dramatized their dramatic situation and their hopes:

> For seven days the lifeboats sailed on, and the starving men eat their fragment of biscuit and their morsel of pork in the morning, and hungrily counted the tedious hours until noon

and night should bring their repetitions of it. And in the long intervals they looked mutely into each other's faces, or turned their wistful eyes across the wild sea in search of the succoring sail that was never to come ... they did not talk, they were too down-hearted. (Branch 172)

Mark Twain said of his hastily written *Hornet* letter:

We got through with this work at six in the evening. I took no dinner, for there was no time to spare if I would beat the other correspondents. I spent four hours arranging the notes in their proper order, then wrote all night and beyond it; with this result: that I had a very long and detailed account of the *Hornet* episode ready at nine in the morning, while the correspondents of the San Francisco journals had nothing but a brief outline report, for they didn't sit up. (qtd. in Taylor 13)

The schooner *Milton Badger* was to sail for San Francisco at nine that morning. Mark Twain managed to finish the article and stuff it into a large envelope, throwing it upon the deck of the departing schooner *Milton Badger* that was free forward and just casting off her sternline to sail toward California that morning. He was victorious over his rival correspondents. Twain's scoop made page one of the Union and ran three and a half columns, and it was telegraphed to Eastern papers: "He became about the best-known honest man on the Pacific Coast" (Day, *Letters* vi).

"The *Hornet* disaster is a classic tale of catastrophe and courage, one of perennial interest to students of maritime history..." (Stone 142). Mark Twain's comment about the event reflects his experience:

> My article was about the burning of the clipper-ship *Hornet* on the line, May 3, 1866. There were thirty-one men on board at the time, and I was in Honolulu when the fifteen lean and ghostly survivors arrived after a voyage of forty-three days in an open boat, through the blazing tropics, on ten days' rations of food ... In those early days I had already published one little thing: 'The Jumping Frog,' in an Eastern paper, but I did not consider that counted ... I spent four hours arranging the notes in their proper order, then wrote all night and beyond it with this result: that I had a very long and detailed account of the *Hornet* episode ready at nine in the morning, while the correspondents of the San Francisco journals had nothing but a brief outline report--for they didn't sit up ... it was my complete report which made the stir and was telegraphed to the New York papers. (qtd. in Taylor 13)

Mark Twain played up the macabre aspects of the longboat adventure for all they were worth. In this first report he gave his fragmentary version of the disaster:

> A letter arrived here to Honolulu yesterday morning giving a meager account of the arrival on the island of Hawaii of nineteen poor starving wretches, who had been buffeting a

> stormy sea in an open boat for forty-three days! Their ship, the *Hornet*, from New York, with a quantity of kerosene on board, had taken fire and burned in latitude two degrees and longitude 135 degrees west. Think of their sufferings for forty-three days and nights, exposed to the scorching heat of the center of the torrid zone, and at the mercy of a ceaseless storm! When they had been entirely out of provisions for a day or two and the cravings of hunger became insupportable, they yielded to the shipwrecked mariner's final and tearful alternative, and solemnly drew lots to determine who of their number should die to furnish food for his comrades. (qtd. in Stone 145)

Twain further states that the *Hornet* survivors reached the Sandwich Islands on the 15th of June:

> They were mere skinny skeletons; their clothes hung limp about them and fitted them no better than a flag fits a flagstaff in a calm. But they were well nursed in a hospital; the people of Honolulu kept them supplied with all the dainties they could need; they gathered strength fast, and were presently nearly as good as new. (qtd. in Taylor 14)

The *Hornet* dispatch to the *Union* was widely reprinted and talked about and brought Mark Twain a new kind of fame as a straight news reporter. The letter is one of his best accomplishments in dramatic reporting, and makes convincing use of physical and psychological detail, even though it was quickly assembled.

Hoping to parlay his fame into something more literary he reworked the *Hornet* material for another article: "Forty-three Days in an Open Boat," Harper's *Magazine*, December, 1866. Because of its intrinsic interest and because his own career was so intimately tied to it, the story of the *Hornet* and its courageous captain haunted Mark Twain. In the late 1890's, as he began to compose his autobiography, one of the first chapters was called "My Debut as a Literary Person." This essay, which discussed the importance of the *Hornet* letters in his career, appeared first in Richard Watson Gilder's *Century Magazine*, November, 1899. He would humorously recall that even in his literary debut, the magazine had listed him as the author Mark Swain (Kaplan 63). But destiny had begun. An appointment with dreams and circumstance had enabled a new literary person to make their debut on the American scene with stories about Hawaii.

The young Mark Twain

CHAPTER TWO

MARK TWAIN IN PARADISE

On a certain bright day the Islands hove in sight, lying low on the lonely sea ... the imposing promontory of Diamond Head rose up out of the ocean its rugged front softened by the hazy distance, and presently the details of the land began to make themselves manifest: first the line of the beach; then the plumed coconut trees... (qtd. in Day, *Letters* 2)

The above passage was Mark Twain's initial reaction to paradise in: *Hawaii-Roughing It in the Sandwich Islands*, with a foreword by A. Grove Day, former Twain specialist at the University of Hawaii (Day, *Letters* 2).

In a reprint of a June 1910 letter that Mark Twain wrote to *The New York Tribune*, in 1873, *Paradise of the Pacific Magazine* refers to Mark Twain's memory of paradise:

You are in the center of the Pacific Ocean; you are two thousand miles from any continent; you are millions of miles from the world; as far as you can see, only land, the crested billows wall the horizon, and beyond this barrier the wide universe is but a foreign land to you, and barren of interest. The climate is simply delicious, never cold at the sea level, and never really too warm, for you are at the half-way house, twenty degrees above the equator ... you drowse your days away in a long dream of peace; the past is a forgotten thing, the present is heaven. You get the idea? (qtd. in Drury 13)

In those days, land travel was largely on horse or mule back over trails; villages or homes were often far apart; there were no telephones, and mails were slow and none too frequent. Mark Twain was a tireless sightseer and began at once his reporting duties by riding around Oahu, the capital of Hawaii on a spavine horse. He had flaming red hair and a drooping mustache. His usual attire was a brown linen duster, heavily starched, that reached to his ankles. "He talked and gesticulated so much that people who did not know him thought he was always drunk" (qtd. in Day, *Letters* 6). His trips from Oahu to Maui and Hawaii were conducted on the principle of going everywhere and seeing everything. He traveled one month through Oahu, and visited historical sites and "show" places. He rode up the Nuuanu and Kalihi Valleys and took the trip around the island. He then spent five weeks on the neighboring island of Maui. While on Maui he climbed to Haleakala Crater's summit and also saw Iao Valley. Next he took a voyage on a schooner to the Kona Coast, staying three weeks on the Big Island where he is reported to have planted a monkeypod tree at Waiohinu (Day, 6). He climbed the Kilauea Volcano district, crossing the crater's lava crust floor. Afterward he visted the sugar plantations of the Hamakua region, collecting and transmitting detailed statistics not only about the sugar industry, but also about the whaling industry. While there he realized the commercial importance of the Hawaiian Islands. Finally Mark Twain rode along Waipio Valley, went across Waimea tableland, and then returned to Honolulu on Oahu, spending a final month there before boarding the small steamer Kilauea for the return trip to San Francisco.

The islands Await Mark Twain

A vein of iron runs through *The Hawaiian Letters*. The author had a vigorous mind, a sharp pen, and much wit. One can almost read *The Hawaiian Letters* with a sense of discovery. The letters were the young journalist's first effort to write up a foreign people and culture, and the author appeared to have promise. His correspondence seemed to have three purposes: he wanted to report the Hawaiian industry and trade with particular reference to American enterprise; he wanted to explain the islands and their populations, including the natives' surroundings, customs, and traditions; he wanted to amuse his readers with the personal, sensational, and fictitious to catch the eager interest of Californians in the romantic islands (Branch 161). Twain sprinkled his travel letters with the workings of a vivid imagination. His letters reflect a transitional state in his work, for they are neither fiction or journalism, but a little of each. There are three letters on Hawaiian trade and industry, and at times these three letters became semi-technical. Mark Twain tried to convey the islands' commercial potentialities and urged their fullest exploitation by Californians. He had the ability to assemble the facts about Hawaiian trade with clarity and force. The insights he demonstrated toward social and economic realities would shape moral judgments he passed on in future writings, especially those writings dealing with social and economic conditions of his fellow man. The trade letters reveal some of his working assumptions about the social order, and measure some of his maturity as a sociologist and moralist at this time (Branch 173).

He believed that duties should be lowered, and favored the influx of Americans into the islands. He felt a regular steamship service should be established between Honolulu and California, and that California should make a bid for the whaling trade considering that the profits in whaling were potentially great. The letter on the sugar industry has wider implications. He felt that it was California's destiny to develop the Hawaiian sugar trade, thus promoting prosperity and trade on nationwide scale. Early Hawaiian sugar acres produced thirteen thousands pounds of sugar with a potential over the islands of twenty-seven million pounds to two billion pounds of sugar (Vandercook 13).

Even though he was an ardently patriotic Californian and felt that the destinies of California and the Hawaiian Islands were linked, Mark Twain did indeed love the Pacific Islands. He shared his sense of the unfamiliar with his readers, and filled out the letters with descriptive and narrative material: "I would rather smell Honolulu at sunset," he wrote, "than the old Police courtroom in San Francisco" (Day, *Letters* 12). In the eighth letter to the *Union* he mentioned the islanders who "always squat on their hams and who knows but they may be the original 'ham sandwiches'" (Frear 297). He also liked the "demoralizing hula" which was forbidden "save at night," with closed doors, but he became almost lyrical about the beauty of Hawaii. In the fourth letter to *The Sacramento Union*, Mr. Brown would remind the author that in Honolulu there were "more centipedes and scorpions and spiders and mosquitoes and missionaries" than anywhere else in the world" (Frear 278).

The city of Honolulu had "streets from twenty to thirty feet wide, solid and level as a floor, most of them straight as a line and a few as crooked as a corkscrew..." (Frear 275). On one moonlight night, Mark Twain left his American hotel on an excursion to Diamond Head and the king's coconut grove. He mentions halting on the summit of a hill which commanded a far reaching view. The moon rose and "flooded the mountain and valley and ocean with a mellow radiance, and out of the shadows of the foliage the distant lights of Honolulu glinted like an encampment of fireflies. The air was heavy with the fragrance of flowers" (qtd. in Clemens, *Honolulu Star* 3).

Twain continues giving voice to his thoughts:

> What a picture is here slumbering in the solemn glory of the moon! How strong the rugged outlines of the dead volcano stand out against the clear sky! What a snowy fringe marks the bursting of the surf over the long, curvy reef! How calmly the dim city sleeps yonder in the plain! How soft the shadows lie upon the stately mountains that border the dream haunted Manoa Valley… (qtd. in Clemens 3)

About this time he wrote his mother and sister in St. Louis:

> I have been here two or three weeks, and like the beautiful tropical climate better and better. I have ridden on horseback all over Oahu and have visited the ancient battlefields and other places of interest. I went with the American minister and took dinner this evening with the king's grand chamberlain, who is related to the royal family. (qtd. in Clemens 4)

Honolulu itself was composed of many different nationalities. Mark Twain wrote of the Hawaiian people that they had excellent characteristics and splendid physiques, that they were hospitable, loved music, religion and education, were experts in the water, and that the girls have "'good home faces'" (Pitchford 35). In his eighth letter, Twain noted that the "native girls by twos and threes and parties of a dozen, and sometimes in whole platoons and companies, went to cantering up and down the neighboring Honolulu streets astride fleet but homely horses, and with their gaudy riding habits streaming like banners behind them" (qtd. in Frear 296).

Mark Twain's descriptions of the Kanaka (native) were often touched with satire. He tried to make this sensational reading (Branch 167). He told the readers that the Kanaka was a fine physical specimen, an able sailor and horseman, hospitable and friendly. He had developed skills in music and dancing, was unselfish and independent in many of his activities, but also superstitious and as was the custom, subservient to authority. The Kanaka was tricky in horse-dealing, an expert in lying, and very uninhibited in sexual relations:

> The natives of the islands number only about fifty thousand, and the whites about three thousand, chiefly Americans ... For nearly a century the natives have been keeping up a ratio of three births to five deaths, and you can see what that must result in. No doubt in fifty years, a Kanaka will be a curiosity in his own land, and as an investment will be superior to a circus. They are about the most interesting savages there are. Their language is soft and musical, and all their words end with a vowel. (Drury 14)

The natives, according to Twain, would make any stranger welcome, and divide their all with him. They lived only for today, not worrying about tomorrow. Twain could not understand where old Kamehameha got his fierce warriors, for the Kanakas of the present are "the most peaceful, inoffensive, unwarlike creatures imaginable. They are wild, free riders, and perfectly at home in the saddle. When a Kanaka rides through the country, he stops fifteen or twenty minutes at every single cabin he comes to and has a chat" (Clemens 4).

Mark Twain discussed the Kanakas' clothing, food, skill in tattooing, and their ancient customs of hiding the bones of dead royalty, of offering human sacrifice, and of granting the right of sanctuary. He had the opportunity to observe, following the death of Princess Victoria, a native mourning rite that included twenty-five natives sitting, densely packed together under the glare of torches. There were hula girls in the center, showily attired in white bodices and pink skirts, and with wreaths of pink and white flowers and garlands of green leaves about their heads.

There were curious moral and religious aspects of the Kanaka prior to the influx of the missionary. Twain believed that their religion was a jumble of curious superstitions. The shark seemed to have been the god they worshipped, and there was Pele, the goddess who presided over the terrible fires of Kilauea. But the Kanaka had been "redeemed by the missionary" (Drury 15).

"The natives used to go naked, but the missionaries broke that up. Men wear clothing in the towns now. Most of the women wear a single loose calico gown (muumuu) that falls without a break from neck to heels." (Drury 14). Twain felt that nothing short of religion could have wrought these admirable changes.

In an early islands letter Twain contrasted the present state of the natives with conditions before they were influenced by missionaries: "How sad it is to think of the multitudes who have gone to their graves in this beautiful island and never knew there was a hell" (Frear 128-48). The main charm of this island paradise for Mark Twain appeared to be his view that the natives were not troubled by a conscience. He viewed them as simple children, and believed they were worse off now that four missionary denominations had "landed there" (Branch 150).

Mark Twain's thinking on the missionaries exhibits some interesting parallels. He displayed a keen interest in the Hawaiian missions, and his concern is understandable. He was always interested in the ethical and religious state of man, and could not fail to "assess a public experiment undertaken for man's spiritual betterment" (Branch 177). While Mark Twain condemned the missionaries, he also found some merit with them. While he called them bigoted, puritanical, slow, and uncharitable toward the weaknesses of the flesh, he also believed they had brought the blessings of progress and civilization to the natives. The end justified the means. They had helped eradicate the control of the King, priests, and tribal chiefs--a control that included maintaining poverty, superstitious tabu, human sacrifice, and feudal subservience. Despite their shortcomings, Mark Twain believed the missionaries had helped destroy this old system and liberate the common man. Branch says that Twain, on his way back to San Francisco, wrote that the missionaries had "made honest men out of a nation of thieves; instituted marriage; created homes and lifted women to the same rights and privileges enjoyed elsewhere" (Branch 177).

The Hawaiian dwellings visited by Twain were ornamented by a hundred species of beautiful flowers and blossoming shrubs, and shaded by noble tamarind trees and the Pride of India with its fragrant flowers, and by the Umbrella Tree, and I do not know how many more..." (Day, *Aloha* 46). Much fresh fruit was available, and Twain "indulged freely" (Day, *Aloha* 46). He also attended a hula and said in his sixteenth letter the "lascivious dance was wont to set the passions of men ablaze in the old heathen days, a century ago" (qtd. In Frear 351).

Mildred Clemens, cousin of Mark Twain, interviewed a Peter Cushman Jones, who remembered cashing Samuel Clemens' monthly check for $100 from *The Union* (M. Clemens, *Sunset Magazine* 96). Mark Twain discovered he was a man of importance in Hawaii and that he was on an assignment that gave him prestige. Because of this advantage he associated with people he most likely would not have known on the mainland. He had the exciting opportunity to visit the king (Emerson 32-33).

The royal palace was described as "a large, roomy framed building," and he described the King, Kamehameha V, in the seventeenth letter as follows:

The King is thirty-four years of age, it is said, but looks all of fifty. He has an observant, inquiring eye, a heavy, massive face, a lighter complexion than is common with his race, tolerably short, stiff hair, a moderate mustache, and imperial, large stature, inclining somewhat to corpulence ... has fleshy hands but a small foot for his size, is about six feet high, is thoughtful and slow of movement, and is a better man and a better-looking one than he is represented to be in the villainous popular photographs of him, for none of them are good. (qtd. in Frear 36)

Hawaiian Royalty

Twain further recalled: "There was no trivial royal nonsense about him; he dressed plainly, poked about Honolulu night and day on his old horse, unattended; he was popular, greatly respected, and even beloved" (qtd. in Day, *Letters* 8).

Unlike the Kanaka people, Mark Twain found the nobility to be educated, fine-looking people. They seemed to have large stature and commanding presence. His endorsement of the nobility is one indication of his strong paternalism in his letters. He observed that the King, his ministers, and his nobles were the political masters of the impotent parliament. The King possessed almost absolute authority, and Twain felt this was just as well, since that King was a man of good sense and education (Branch 167).

There were only two things Mark Twain did not like about Hawaii. One was raw fish, of which he said: "Let's change the subject," and the other was poi: "It smells a good deal worse than it looks. It is a villianous mixture, almost tasteless before it ferments and too sour for luxury afterwards" (qtd. in Pitchford 35). He enumerated further about poi:

> Nothing in the world is more nutritious ... many a different finger goes into the same bowl ... one tall gentleman, with nothing in the world on but a soiled and greasy shirt, thrust in his finger ant tested the poi, shook his head, scratched it with the useful finger, made another test, prospected among his hair, caught something and ate it; tested the poi again, wiped the grimy perspiration from his brow with the

universal hand, tested again, blew his nose--'Let's move on, Brown,' I said. (Frear 47)

Mark Twain's letters to *The Union* about Honolulu abounded in genuine good humor and fun. His vivid description in his fourth letter of the cats, mosquitoes, and "centipedes," which he encountered in Honolulu follows:

> I saw cats--Tom cats, Mary Ann cats, long-tailed cats, bob-tail cats, blind cats, one-eyed cats, wall-eyed cats, cross-eyed cats, gray cats, black cats, white cats, yellow cats, striped cats, spotted cats, tame cats, wild cats, singed cats, individual cats, groups of cats, platoons of cats, companies of cats, regiments of cats, armies of cats, multitudes of cats, millions of cats, and all of them sleek, fat, lazy and sound asleep; in place of roughs and rowdies staring and sound asleep. (qtd. in Frear 276-77)

Mildred Clemens recalls a humorous story about Twain's recollection of the cats. During one of her visits to Hawaii, she tells of someone telling her about a young and unknown man walking into the office of *The Commercial Advertiser* and offering an article to the editor for publication. After the stranger had left, the editor began reading the above discourse on Honolulu cats, and became annoyed, remarking the young fellow who left the article must have been crazy, that he (the editor) had never seen the large number of cats described in the article. Little did the editor know that the article he crumbled and tossed in the wastebasket and later retrieved would come to light later as one of the immortal writings of that "crazy" young man--Mark Twain (Clemens 4). To offended cat lovers, Mildred Clemens notes that Mark Twain was indeed fond of cats, and had a cat as a child that sat by him at the table and ate from his own plate (Clemens 4).

The centipedes were another favorite topic, as his imaginary traveling companion, Mr. Brown, notes in the fourth letter:

> You get nipped by one of them scorpions once, and see how you like it! And you want to know what made me light out of bed so sudden last night? Only a 'centipede'--nothing, only a 'centipede,' with forty-two legs on a side, and every foot hot enough to burn a hole through a raw-hide. (Frear 277-78)

Brown continued his tirade of complaints to Mark Twain:

> You look at them raw splotches all over my face--all over my arms--all over my body! Mosquito bites! Don't tell me about mere--mere things! You can't get around them mosquitoes ... I was in bed the other night and they swarmed in there and jammed their bills through my shirt and sucked me as dry as a life-preserver before I got my breath again. (Frear 278)

Despite discussing the negative aspects of island living, Mark Twain would much later write in *The New York Daily Tribune*, January 9, 1873:

> Let us annex the Islands. Think how we could build up that whaling trade. Let us annex. We could make sugar enough

here to supply all America perhaps, and the prices would be very easy with the duties removed ... we could raise cotton and coffee there and make it pay pretty well ... we could own the mightiest volcano on earth--Kiluea! Let us annex, by all means ... we could put the savages on a reservation--a reservation where they have annual hoes, Bibles and blankets to trade for powder and whiskey--a sweet Arcadian retreat fenced in with soldiers. By annexing, we would get all those fifty thousand natives cheap as dirt, with their morals and other diseases thrown in. No expense for education--they are already educated; no need to convert them--for they are already converted; no expense to clothe them--for obvious reasons. We must annex those people. We can afflict them with our wise and beneficent government ... our thieves and political influence. We can make them ashamed of their simple and primitive justice ... we can give them lecturers. I will go myself. We can make that little bunch of sleepy islands the hottest corner on earth, and array it in the moral splendor of our high and holy civilization. Annexation is what the poor islanders need. Shall we to men benighted, the lamp of life deny. (qtd. In Horton 94)

During his four weeks or so on Oahu before going to the other islands, Mark Twain wrote his first eleven letters to *The Union*, and diligently continued his study of Hawaiian. At the end of his twelfth letter from the Sandwich Islands Twain confessed that he had not touched a pen for six weeks. He had gone to visit the "somnolent island of Maui" (Day, *Aloha* 46). Although he intended to stay in Maui one week, he stayed five, and would later remember Maui as a dream refuge from pressures that go with being a celebrity, and "had never spent so pleasant a month before, or bade any place goodbye so regretfully" (Clemens 5).

He rode horseback all over Maui wearing a long, linen duster with the tails flapping in the wind. Doctor Carl B. Andrews related the following story:

> While in Wailuku, Maui, Twain had his own cottage, part of the time, and mornings would appear outside the garden in his linen duster. The neighborhood women began to suspect that the garment represented his sole raiment, and determined to find out. So one morning, as if by accident when using the hose next door, they accidentally let it turn on Twain. This proved their suspicions, and poor Mark never suspected their real intent while accepting their profuse apologies. (Clemens 5)

Maui boasts two extraordinary features of scenic interest: the Iao Valley and the extinct volcano Haleakala. While visiting Maui, Twain toured the green, lush valley of Iao, and climbed the 10,000-foot-high Haleakala Volcano, called "The House of the Sun." He was embraced by the grandeur of the valley, and it was there that his "My Platonic Sweetheart" would have its setting. The Iao Valley was "a verdure-clad needle of stone, a thousand feet high, stepped out from behind a corner, and mounted guard over the mysteries of the valley." (Frear 59) Twain was most impressed by the chief pride of Maui ... her dead volcano, Haleakala. He wrote one letter home titled "Wailuku, Sugar Plantation, Island of Maui, Hawaii, May 4, 1866." It was 11:00 p.m. when he wrote the letter, and he continued:

> This is the infernalist darkest country, when the moon don't shine ... I have been clattering around among the plantations for three weeks, now, and I am going to visit the extinct crater of Mount Haleakala, the largest in the world; it is 10 miles to the foot of the mountain; it rises 10,000 feet above the valley; the crater is 29 miles in circumference and 1,000 feet deep. Seen from the summit, the city of St. Louis would look like a picture in the bottom of it. (qtd. in M. Clemens 5)

After viewing the crater, Twain wrote:

> The impressive scene overawed speech. A growing warmth suffused the horizon and soon the sun emerged and looked out over the cloud waste, flinging bars of ruddy light across it, staining its folds and hollow caps with blushes, purpling the shaded troughs between, and glorifying the many vapor palaces and cathedrals with a wasteful splendor of all blending and combinations of rich coloring. (Pitchford 36)

Twain's viewing of the Haleakala crater made such a lasting impression on him that five years later in the middle of writing *Roughing It*, at Quarry Farm in Elmira, New York, Mark Twain was to say: "It was the sublimest spectacle I ever witnessed, and I think the memory of it will stay with me always. I felt like the Last Man, neglected of judgment, and left pinnacled in mid-heaven, a forgotten relic of a vanished world" (M. Clemens 5).

Near the beautiful gorge of Iao on Maui is Wailuku, according to Mildred Clements, Twain remembers in *Roughing It*:

> I still remember, with a sense of indolent luxury, a picnicking excursion up a romantic gorge there, called the Iao Valley ... Presently, a verdure-clad needle of stone, a thousand feet high, stepped out from behind a corner, and mounted guard over the mysteries of the valley ... It was in that beautiful valley that I saw an original grass house, some real, original Hawaiians and something of their life as Mark Twain saw it and as comparatively few see it nowadays. Like the sequoias of California standing serene upon a geological island, survivors of a previous epoch, these gentle natives, at the time of my visit, appeared in a sea of racial cross breeding. (M. Clemens, "Mark Twain" 5)

On May 22, Mark was back in Honolulu and writing home to his sister. He wrote:

> I have just got back from a sea voyage-from the beautiful island of Maui. I have spent five week there, riding backwards and forwards among the sugar plantations--looking up the splendid scenery and visiting the lofty crater of Haleakala. It has been a perfect jubilee to me in the way of pleasure ... I have not written a single line, and have not once thought of business or care or human toil or trouble or

sorrow or weariness. Few such months come in a lifetime. (qtd. in M. Clemens, "Mark Twain" 9)

One week later Mark Twain set sail for the big island of Hawaii to see the great active volcano of Kilauea. One day Captain Ezra Dane was at the pier in Honolulu when a man came down to the dock and asked where the boat went? When the young gentleman found out the boat was sailing to the big island he left, then soon returned with an old-fashioned carpet bag and booked passage. On the voyage the cook took sick and the captain tried to make biscuits. Mark Twain wrote, "His intentions were good, but his biscuits were damnable" (Clemens 6). One needs only to look through the pages of *Roughing It*, volume two, written five years after his island visit, to see the vivid impressions the visit to the Big Island made on him. To Mark Twain, the dreamer, it was a new, strange, fascinating world. He first visited the Kona district, having landed at Kailua. He rode horseback through the region. He tells us in *Roughing It*:

> The trail passes along on high ground--say a thousand feet above sea level- and usually about a mile distant from the ocean, which is always in sight, save that occasionally you find yourself buried in the forest in the midst of a rank tropical vegetation and a dense growth of trees, whose great boughs over-arch tunnel, haunted with invisible singing birds and fragrant with the odor of flowers. (Twain 908)

Kona coffee had a richer flavor to him than any he had ever tasted, and he insisted that there were no finer oranges produced in the world than those grown in Kona. The principal market for those oranges, incidentally, was California, which at that time imported about a million and a half pounds of oranges from Kona.

Mark Twain's cousin, Mildred Clemens, visited the same area as Mark Twain did when she vacationed on the big island of Hawaii in 1916. She met a Mrs. Coon, who told her the following story about Mark Twain, who had visited at her father's plantation on the Big Island:

> A gentleman who gave his name as Clemens had come to the plantation and after the custom of those days had asked if he might stay there for a time. He was most welcome and proved a delightful guest. But father was Scotch and essentially practical and farming on a recent lava flow was hard digging. Our guest took life a little too easily, I suppose, and one day my father said to mother, somewhat testily, 'I wonder who that duffer is? He's too lazy to hoe a row of potatoes.' After awhile Mr. Clemens (for such he had introduced himself) went away, without having reformed. One day there came an autographed copy of an article by 'Mark Twain' acknowledging our hospitality and giving a beautiful description of our place which he called 'an oasis in the desert.' Father scratched his head when he saw the signature, then said, much mollified. 'So that was Mark Twain!' (for that name did mean something to us), then added, with the old spirit, 'Well, anyhow, he was too lazy to hoe a row of potatoes!' (M. Clemens, "Mark Twain" 6)

Kealakekua Bay

Later Twain visited Kealakekua Bay where Captain Cook, discoverer of the Islands in 1778, was killed, and writes of this memorable experience:

> As the red sun looked across the placid ocean through the tall, clean stems of the coconut trees, like a blooming whiskey bloat through the bars of a city prison, I went and stood in the edge of the water on the flat rock pressed by Captain Cook's feet when the blow was dealt that took away his life, and tried to picture in my mind the doomed man struggling in the midst of the multitude of exasperated savages--the men in the ship crowding to the vessel's side and gazing in anxious dismay toward the shore--the--But I discovered that I could not do it... (Grant 31)

In writing his long record of Captain Cooke's experiences and death in the islands, Mark Twain was helped greatly by James

Jarves' history. Cooke's story is told with vivacity and interest, with no farces or digressions that appear in many of the letters. He appeared critical toward Cooke's activities and seemed to have a humanitarian sympathy for the island natives. He believed that they had been cruelly wronged by Cooke's deceptions and his use of force. The subject of Captain Cooke stimulated some of the most vivid and fast-moving prose in the letters.

In his 22nd letter to *The Sacramento Union*, dated from Kealakekua Bay, Hawaii, July, 1866, Twain describes the ruins of the City of Refuge (Frear 395). At noon his group hired a Kanaka (man) to take them in a canoe four miles down the coast to Honaunau, the chief City of Refuge, which anciently served as did the cities of refuge of the Old Testament (Frear 68).

The Puuhonua O Honaunau National Historical Park is still an honored place in Hawaii today. It is an ancient, partially restored ruin originally built over 400 years ago. In those days, legend goes, many chiefs ruled in the islands; and each territory had a spot designated as a place of refuge to which kapu breakers, war refugees, and defeated warriors could escape. They could be cleansed of their offenses and return, purified (Hammel 305).

According to Twain, the City of Refuge was a "vast enclosure, whose stone walls were twenty feet thick at the base, and fifteen or twenty feet high ... Within this enclosure, in early times, have been three rude temples; each was 210 feet long by 100 wide, and 13 feet high... (qtd. in Frear 395).

If a man killed another anywhere on the island, the relatives of the deceased could take the murderer's life. The outlawed criminal could then run through forests and over high mountains hoping to enter the protecting walls of the City of Refuge. Once within the walls, a confession could be made to the priest and absolution obtained. The murderer with a price on his head could go forth without fear or without danger. It was tabu to harm him. To do so meant death (Frear 395).

Twain's version of one legend of the City of Refuge reflects his humorous views of human nature. He mentions that fifty or sixty years ago the proud Queen Kaahumanu flew to a rock for safety when she had caused trouble with her husband and then proceeded to hide under the rock until King Kamehameha's anger was appeased. Twain says the legend is a lie because Queen Kaahumanu was six feet high, bulky and built like an ox and that she could no more have squeezed under the rock (at the City of Refuge) than she could have passed between the cylinders of a sugar mill. "What could she gain by it, even if she succeeded? To be chased and abused by her savage husband could not be otherwise than humiliating to her high spirit, yet it could never make her feel so flat as an hour's repose under that rock would" (qtd. in Frear 396). These descriptions appeared in the *Union* letters and later in *Roughing It*.

The stranger on the big island of Hawaii rode into the quiet village of Waiohinu, a small locale that nestled in the warm curved arm of a grassy hill on the lower edge of Mauna Loa. He was tired, and he wanted food. He saw the little white cottage and its beautiful garden; and its refreshing atmosphere invited him to ask the cottage's owner where he might obtain lodging for the night. "My name is Samuel Clemens, and I'm sort of knocking about seeing the country" (qtd. in Rothwell 9). "My father's name was Captain Nelson Haley, and he told the gentlemen that there were no hotels in our district, but that he would be happy to have him stay with us as long as he liked ... It was not until our guest had gone--and in fact--had left the Islands--that we learned of his identity" (Rothwell 9).

Rothwell continues: "Sometimes the stranger talked of his travels. At other times he sat in the garden busy with pen and paper. My mother thought they were letters to his family" (Rothwell 10). It was in this garden that Twain supposedly planted the Saman Tree (Monkeypod).

Why did Mark Twain plant a Monkeypod Tree there in the sleepy, picturesque little town of Waiohinu? Mildred Clemens, a cousin of Mark Twain, wrote 20 chapters in *The Honolulu Star Bulletin* beginning December 7, 1935, and ending December 30, 1935. In these articles she retraced Mark Twain's chronological trip about the islands and made the following observation:

> I decided that maybe that was about as near to paradise he would ever come and wanted to do a little cultivating in that Garden of Eden. At any rate, it wasn't an apple tree! No, but a Monkeypod Tree! Today it spreads its great shade limbs far over the 'around the island' belt road ... And what a contrast is that highway today to the rough and rugged route

followed by Mark Twain in his search for writing material and with a keen desire to 'go places, and do things,' in the common parlance of today. (qtd. in M. Clemens 7)

Most likely Twain did not realize then that the tiny sapling would grow to the huge tree it is today, a "fitting parallel to his fame and glory" (Clemens, Mildred 7). Mildred Clemens would remark: "While trailing Mark Twain over three continents I have seen many monuments erected to his memory, but none, it seems, would please him quite like that spreading Monkeypod Tree in the land, to him always, Paradise!" (M. Clemens 8). An article in the 1936 issue of *Paradise of the Pacific* states: "Residents of Hawaii can journey to Waiohinu and there gaze upon Hawaii's living monument to this memory. It may have been a small tree when he planted that Monkey-pod, but it is a giant today" (Rothwell 9). Unfortunately, the Monkey-pod Tree was destroyed by a windstorm in 1957. After planting the tree, Mark Twain made plans the next day for a riding excursion. "The next day," Twain says, "we bought horses and bent our way over the summer-clad mountain terraces, toward the great volcano of Kilauea (Ke-low-way-ah) ... Shortly, the crater came into view" (qtd. in M. Clemens 5).

Twain saw the goddess Pele in action at the Kilauea Crater, which rises on the southeastern slopes of Mauna Loa (the largest mountain in the world), more than 32,000 feet from sea floor to summit, 18,000 of them below sea level (Hammel 296).
In his twentieth-fourth letter, he brilliantly painted word-pictures of beauty and terror at Kilauea:

> We came upon a long dreary desert of black swollen, twisted, corrugated billows of lava--blank and dismal desolation ... it was a petrified sea ... We came at last to torn and ragged deserts of scorched and blistered lava-- to plains and patches of dull gray ashes--to the summit of the mountain, and these tokens warned us that we were nearing the palace of the dread goddess Pele, the crater of Kilauea. (Frear 415)

The crater was not in violent eruption at the time he saw it, but the sight was enough to turn Twain's humor into a serious vein. He mentions a heavy fog over the crater, illuminated by the glare from the fires below. The illumination was two miles wide and a mile high and Twain was impressed. He states in his twenty-fifth letter from the Sandwich Islands, dated June 3, midnight, from the Volcano House:

> I suppose no man ever saw Niagara for the first time without feeling disappointed. I suppose no man ever saw it the fifth time without wondering how he could ever have been so blind and stupid as to find any excuse for disappointment in the first place. I suppose that any one of nature's most celebrated wonders will always look rather insignificant to a visitor at first, but on a better acquaintance will swell and stretch out and spread abroad, until it finally grows clear beyond his grasp--becomes too stupendous for his comprehension ... I was disappointed when I saw the great volcano of Kilauea today for the first time ... and I reflected

that night was the proper time to view the volcano ... after a hearty supper we waited until it was thoroughly dark and then started to the crater. The first glance in that direction revealed a scene of wild beauty. There was heavy fog over the crater and it was splendidly illuminated by the glare from the fires below. The illumination was two miles wide and a mile high, perhaps; and if you ever, on a dark night and at a distance beheld the light from thirty or forty blocks of distant buildings all on fire at once, reflected strongly against overhanging clouds, you can form a fair idea of what this looked like ... the view was a startling improvement over my daylight experience ... in the strong light every countenance glowed like red-hot iron, every shoulder was suffused with crimson and shaded rearward into dingy, shapeless obscurity! The place below looked like the infernal regions and these men like half-cooled devils just come up from a furlough ... here was room for imagination to work ... you could not compass it--it was the idea of eternity made tangible--and the longest end of it made visible to the naked eye! (qtd. in Abramson 227-30)

Twain saw a colossal column of cloud towering to a great height in the air immediately above the crater, and he mentions that every one of its vast folds was dyed with a rich crimson luster, which was subdued to a pale rose tint in the depressions between. "It glowed like a muffled torch and stretched upward to a dizzy height toward the zenith" (Frear 419). In the twentieth-fifth letter Mark Twain also mentions that he saw color "a dazzling white just tinged with yellow, boiling and surging furiously ... with holes branching into numberless bright torrents, like the 'spokes' of a lady's fan" (qtd. in Abramson 228).

Mildred Clemens also notes the impact of this event on Mark Twain:

> I thought it just possible that its like had not been seen since the children of Israel wandered on their long march through the desert so many centuries ago over a path illuminated by the mysterious 'pillar of fire.' And I was sure that I now had a vivid conception of what the majestic 'pillar of fire' was like, which almost amounted to a revelation. (qtd. in Clemens, Mildred 5)

Twain would travel in the islands for almost another month and would not return to them for almost thirty years, but he would never forget this extraordinary vision of the goddess Pele at work at Kilauea. "I felt like the Last Man, neglected of the Judgment and left pinnacled in mid-heaven, a forgotten relic of a vanished world" (qtd. in M. Clemens, *Sunset Magazine* 7).

Mark Twain also found snowbanks on the summit of Mauna Kea, and said:

> While you shiver in your furs you may cast your eye down the sweep of the mountain side and tell exactly where the frigid zone ends and the vegetable life begins; a stunted and tormented growth of trees shade down into a taller and freer

> species, and that in turn, into the full foliage and varied tints of the temperate zone ... so you perceive, you can look down upon all the climates of the earth, and note the kinds and colors of all the vegetations, just with a glance of the eye--and this glance only travels over about three miles as the bird flies, too. (qtd. in Frear 490)

Saturday of that week, Twain paid a visit to Onomea Plantation with his fictional friend, Mr. Brown. Mr. Clemens bore a letter of introduction which he presented to the owner of the plantation, a Mr. Austin. In the middle of the conversation it was discovered that the visitor was also Mark Twain. As Mr. Austin says:

> In those days many tourists came that way, having a desire to see the place where Capt. Cook was killed, then riding overland to the volcano, thence departing by way of Hilo. This is what Samuel Clemens did, only he did not depart from Hilo but rode on to Kawaihae, about 80 miles further around the island, before taking vessel. Why he chose to take this fearfully hard ride over the gulches I am sure I cannot say and he fails to explain. (M. Clemens, "Mark Twain" 9)

Perhaps the answer can be explained by Mark Twain's biographer, Paine, who says that any new place in those days filled Clemens with an insatiable desire to see it. This urge no doubt made him continue on around the island (M. Clemens 9).

After his trip to the big island, Twain wrote:

> I have just got back from a hard trip through the island of Hawaii, begun on the 26th of May and finished on the 8th of June ... I stayed at the volcano about a week and witnessed the greatest eruption that has occurred for years. I lived well there. They charge $4 a day for board and a dollar or two extra for guides and horses. I had a pretty good time. They didn't charge me anything (for that)... (qtd. in M. Clemens 9)

Immediately after this excursion Mark Twain returned to Honolulu where he had scored his news scoop about the *Hornet* survivors in his fifteenth letter to *The Union*. He had the friendship of Ambassador Burlingame to thank for the scoop and was always humbly grateful, later writing that Burlingame was a man who could be "esteemed, respected and popular anywhere" (M. Clemens 9).

Mark Twain not only owed his *Hornet* story to the assistance of Burlingame, but also his new outlook on life. Burlingame's example, companionship, and advice came at a crucial time in Mark Twain's youth. The following advice that Burlingame gave to Twain would affect him his whole life: "Associate more with persons of refinement and intellect ... Seek companionship among men of superior intellect and character. Refine yourself and your work. Never affiliate with inferiors; always climb" (Ferguson 110).

Twain's biographer, Paine, also agrees that Burlingame's mentorship had a dramatic effect on Mark Twain's impressionistic youthful mind:

Burlingame's example, companionship and advice, coming when it did, were in the nature of a revelation to Samuel Clemens, who returned to San Francisco, consciously or not, the inhabitant of a new domain. (Paine, *Speeches* xii)

Burlingame also called Twain a genius and complimented him highly on his talent.

"As it was, Twain accepted the advice (and compliments) gratefully and treasured it the rest of his life. If it did nothing else, it strengthened his hunch that he must move from California to the East if he was to establish himself as something more than a humorist" (Gerber 20). It also gave him the aspiration of moving to a place in the world "higher than that of a California journalist" (Ferguson 110).

Frear, in Appendix C, lists the Letters in the order they appeared in *The Daily Union*:

1. On Board *Ajax*, March 18, printed daily April 16, weekly April 21
2. Honolulu, March 19, 1866, printed daily April 17, weekly April 21
3. Honolulu, March, 1866, printed daily April 18, weekly April 21
4. Honolulu, March, 1866, printed daily April 19, weekly April 21
5. Honolulu, March, 1866, printed daily April 20, weekly April 21

6. Honolulu, March, 1866, printed daily April 21, weekly April 28
7. Honolulu, March, 1866, printed daily April 24, weekly April 28
8. Honolulu, April, 1866, printed daily May 21, weekly May 26
9. Honolulu, April, 1866, printed daily May 22, weekly May 26
10. Honolulu, April, 1866, printed daily May 23, weekly May 26
11. Honolulu, April, 1866, printed daily May 24, weekly June 2
12. Honolulu, May 23, 1866, printed daily June 20, weekly June 23
13. Honolulu, May 23, 1866, printed daily June 21, weekly June 23
14. Honolulu, June 22, 1886, printed daily July 16, weekly July 21
15. Honolulu, June 25, 1866, printed daily July 19, weekly July 21
16. Honolulu, June 30, 1866, printed daily July 30, weekly August 4
17. Honolulu, July 1, 1866, printed daily August 1, weekly August 4
18. Honolulu, July, 1866, printed daily August 18, weekly August 25

19. Kona, Hawaii, July, 1866, printed daily August 24, weekly August 25
20. Kealakekua Bay, Hawaii, 1866, printed daily August 30, weekly September 1
21. Kealakekua Bay, July, 1866, printed daily September 6, weekly September 8
22. Kealakekua Bay, July 1866, printed daily September 22, weekly September 29
23. Honolulu, September 10, 1866, printed daily September 26, weekly September 29
24. Kilauea, June, 1866, printed daily October 25, weekly October 27
25. Volcano House, June3--midnight, printed daily November 16, weekly November 17 (Frear)

In retrospect, the Hawaiian letters are excellent journalism, and are distinguished by an irrepressible flow of high spirits which disarms even the critical reader. There are no pauses in the letters, and all the different journeys attract attention because they reflect the glitter of the young Mark Twain's personality.

Mark Twain would later prepare his Hawaiian letters into a book manuscript, but he was not able to publish it. However, in recent years the original versions have been collected into book form more than one time, beginning in 1920 with only thirty printed copies of *The Sandwich Islands By Mark Twain*, edited by H. C. Quinby. This first known edition was a beautiful 10 x 7 inch volume, and contained Mark Twain's two later letters of 1873 to *The New York*

Tribune, and his lecture on the Sandwich Islands as found in *Modern Eloquence*. Also contained in this edition was a prospectus and a ticket for the New York lecture of May 7, 1867. Sales of this volume in recent years have been from twenty dollars to seventy-five dollars.

Although often reprinted separately, Mark Twain's letters were never collected in book form until the Grabhorn Press in San Francisco published in 1937, with an introduction and conclusion by G. Ezra Dane, a limited edition of 550 copies titled *Letters From the Sandwich Islands* and illustrated by Dorothy Grover (Frear 245). The following year a photo-offset edition was issued by the Stanford University Press. The Dane volume omitted part of Letter Three on Hawaiian trade and all of Letters Ten (whaling), Fifteen (the *Hornet* disaster), and Twenty-three (the sugar industry). These four letters were published in 1939 by Thomas Nickerson of Honolulu, with an introduction by John V. Vandercook; the volume, entitled *Letters from Honolulu*, was limited to one thousand copies and was printed by the Lakeside Press of Chicago. The first complete reprinting appeared as Appendix C of *Mark Twain and Hawaii* (1947), in an excellent study by Walter Francis Frear, well-known judge and third governor of the territory of Hawaii. Frear's book was also published by the Lakeside Press and was limited to one thousand autographed copies. All these editions were expensive and have long been out of print (Day, *Letters* 24, 1966).

Mark Twain also used the letters as the basis of chapters seventy-four through seventy-eight of *Roughing It* (1872), by "drawing on ninety thousand words of his *Union* letters" (Day, *Letters* x). The greater portion of *Roughing It*, written five years after his return to the mainland, incorporated most of Mark Twain's reminiscences of his island vagrancy. The work was written at Quarry Farm ... situated picturesquely on the hillside overlooking the town of Elmira, New York. He had to leave some of the material out because it was too "spirited." Shorter, later versions of the Hawaiian adventures in *Roughing It* are more smoothly written and more artfully told, and the crude Mr. Brown does not appear" (Day, *Letters* xi).

Roughing It is more than a travel book, but almost a fictionalized autobiography, a sketch book of people and places from his 1861-66 experiences, including his visit to the Sandwich Islands. Gerber says that chapters on the Sandwich Island trip were added at the last minute (Gerber 47).

On August 13 Mark Twain wrote in his notebook: "San Francisco, Home again. No, not home again--in prison again and all the wide sense of freedom gone. The city seems so cramped and so dreary with toil and care and business anxiety. God help me, I wish I were at sea again" (qtd. in Ferguson 111). There was no reason for him to be despondent. The humorous and informative letters in *The Union* had vastly increased his fame, and he had also received a $300 bonus for his *Hornet* scoop. He mailed a fuller account of the *Hornet* story to *Harper's Magazine*, and it was quickly accepted. He would later call the publication of this article his "Debut as a Literary Person" (Emerson 34).

Although he did not know it, the Hawaiian experience had in fact determined the pattern that most of his future writing would assume:

> It was the pattern of the Mississippi; motion was its inherent quality. You went on from place to place and wrote about each in its turn. An endless flow of new topics was brought to you; you didn't have to go round a familiar treadmill looking for something to write about. (Ferguson 112)

Twain's writing patterns would become "sublimated and glorified reporting, with no deadlines to meet and no restrictions on subject" (Ferguson 112). Edgar Marquess Branch, in *The Literary Apprenticeship of Mark Twain*, also agrees that the Sandwich Islands letters were a strong part of Mark Twain's literary apprenticeship and helped to determine his future writing patterns:

> We may be sure that the Sandwich Islands letters material contributed to his later travel books and fiction. The training he received was a valuable preliminary to *The Innocents Abroad*, in which also he had to select and recreate the salient features of a region and culture. In *Huckleberry Finn*, a work remote in nearly all respects from the Hawaiian letters, selection and recreation of this sort gave depth and representative quality to his background of river society. (Branch 170-71)

The Sandwich Islands letters were a vital link in Mark Twain's literary career, marking out the characteristic form of his travel books, and to some extent, his fiction. They helped make his name well known, and provided the opportunity as well as the subject for his first lecture tour.

CHAPTER THREE

THE TURNING POINT

"After half a year's luxurious vagrancy in the Islands, I took shipping in a sailing-vessel, and regretfully returned to San Francisco..." (Twain, *Roughing It* 291).

Stephen Leacock said that Mark Twain "returned to San Francisco in a blaze of glory" (Leacock 96-7). That was the beginning of his success as a lecturer, unrivaled except by that of his senior contemporary, Charles Dickens. Twain wanted to conquer the world (Leacock 97).

Upon his return to California, Mark Twain took advantage of his reputation as a Hawaiian authority and decided to lecture on the subject. He says in *Roughing It:* "I was without employment. I tortured my brain for a saving scheme of some kind, and at last a public lecture occurred to me" (Twain, *Roughing It* 953). His lectures, like the letters, would be very comprehensive in subject matter. They covered history, political, educational, social and religious conditions, as well as geography, volcanoes, climate, the sugar and whaling industries, Chinese labor, trade, annexation, steamship communication, land tenure, scenic wonders and beauties, and everything from royalty to "the customs and ways of the common people"

(Frear 183). He especially enjoyed covering the missionaries, whom he regarded as the "biggest liars on earth" (Frear 183). "With his keen power of observation, insight into human nature and absorptive mind he missed almost nothing" (Frear 183). He seasoned his lectures with humor but made them informative as well. "He tried to reach the heart as well as the intellect" (Frear 183).

There are no true preserved manuscripts of the lectures, only newspaper accounts and Mark Twain's memories, but the topic of the Sandwich Islands would be his sole platform subject for a year and a half and "a staple of his repertory for seven--he often billed it 'Our Fellow Savages of the Sandwich Islands'" (Day, *Mark Twain's Letters* xi). On October 2, almost 1,800 people turned out at Maguire's Academy of Music in San Francisco. *The San Francisco Evening-Bulletin* said:

> The Academy of Music was stuffed ... to repletion ... It is perhaps fortunate that the King of Hawaii did not arrive in time to attend, for unless he had gone early he would have been turned away, as many others were who could not gain admittance ... the lecturer then proceeded with his subject, and delivered one of the most interesting and amusing lectures ever delivered in this city... (Frear 437)

Mr. Twain had to pay $50 for renting the hall, and his printing and advertising expenses ran up another $150. Admission price was one dollar. His good friend Bret Harte helped wherever he could (Pitchford 36). Three days before the lecture Mark Twain could not sleep. He described himself as "the most distressed and frightened creature on the Pacific Coast" (Pitchford 36). His lecture brochure said, "Doors open at 7 o'clock; the trouble will begin at 8" (Emerson 35). He later remarked in *Roughing It* that particular line had done such good service that it had been borrowed frequently by showmen and the school system to remind students returning from summer vacation of fall school times. (Twain, *Roughing It* 953). He was greeted with a hurricane of applause from a house that was packed, even in the aisles. He became engulfed by stage fright, spoke his first sentence, recovered, and warmly embraced the crowd. The opening comment was: "Julius Caesar is dead, Shakespeare is dead, Napoleon is dead, Abraham Lincoln is dead, and I am far from well myself" (qtd. in M. Clemens, *The Honolulu Star-Bulletin* 9).

Years later he would describe to an audience his remembrance of his first stage appearance:

> My heart goes out in sympathy to anyone who is making his first appearance before an audience of human beings ... I recall the occasion of my first appearance ... My knees were shaking so that I didn't know whether I could stand up. If there is an awful, horrible malady in the world, it is stage fright and seasickness. They are a pair. I had stage fright then for the first and last time... (qtd. in M. Clemens, *The Honolulu Star-Bulletin* 10)

Mark Twain: Public Speaker

    Twain began to feel apprehensive about his lecture, so he went to three old friends and asked them to sit in the audience and laugh and applaud. He contacted the wife of a popular citizen and asked her and her husband to sit in the left-hand stage box and react with laughter to his speech. He asked a man (who was drinking down the street) that he had never seen before to so the same. He could eat nothing for three days, only suffer. (Twain, *Roughing It* 954). When the time arrived he commented in *Roughing It*:

I went down back streets at six o'clock, and entered the theater by the back door. I stumbled my way in the dark among the ranks of canvas scenery, and stood on the stage. The house was gloomy and silent, and its emptiness depressing. I went into the dark among the scenes again, and for an hour and a half gave myself up to the horrors, wholly unconscious of everything else. Then I heard a murmur; it rose higher and higher, and ended in a crash, mingled with cheers. It made my hair raise, it was so close to me, and so loud. There was a pause, and then another; presently came a third, and before I well knew what I was about, I was in the middle of the stage, staring at a sea of faces, bewildered by the fierce glare of the lights, and quaking in every limb with a terror that seemed like to take my life away. The house was full, aisles and all. (Twain, *Roughing It* 955)

The San Francisco Evening-Bulletin of October 3 pronounced the lecture a brilliant success. *The San Francisco Alta* California of October 3 said that Mark Twain had thoroughly established himself as the most piquant and humorous writer and lecturer on this coast since the days of the lamented. *The San Francisco News Letter* of October 6 said the lecture had one serious fault: it was too short ... the lecture was tip-top ... interesting, instructive ... delivery happy, success complete (Frear 438).

Ferguson in his work, *Mark Twain, Man and Legend*, notes this dramatic moment of Twain's speaking triumph:

> In that hour, on the stage of Maguire's Academy of Music, October 2, 1866, Mark took the last step that was needed to make him one of the greatest writers of the century. He began by infusing into his writing the charm of his drawling speech. Where his writing was crude or stiff, the test of oral utterance exposed the weakness and taught him how to mend it. Though time was still needed to make his finished utterance second nature, his apprenticeship to the craft of letters was complete. Mark Twain the personality had come to birth out of Sam Clemens, and all that he was to say and write for the rest of his life was to be merely an expansion and consolidation of the San Francisco achievement. (Ferguson 113)

Twain's biographer, Paine, says:

> ...the lecture Mark Twain was persuaded to deliver a few months after his return from Hawaii indicates a mental awakening, a growth in vigor and poetic utterance that cannot be measured by comparison with his earlier writings, because it is not of the same realm. (Paine, *Speeches,* xii)

Grant in *Twain* also agrees that the effect of lecturing upon the development of Twain's style cannot be overstressed. Mark Twain's acute ear for speech was immeasurably improved by the time spent in preparing for and practicing on the platform. "His best work was to be written in the language of men rather than of books, and his habit was to write always with the sound of a voice clearly in mind" (Grant 33).

The aftermath of the speaking event was best captured by Mr. Twain: "All the papers were kind in the morning; my appetite returned; I had abundance of money. All's well that ends well" (Twain, *Roughing It* 955).

Mark Twain's books would increase in sales because of his fine readings from them on stage and also because of his stage speeches. He was able, through the spoken medium, also to test unpublished material on his audience, thereby discovering wherein lay the strengths or weaknesses of his writings, as well as get his audience interested in buying the book from this material. The lecture circuit was gratifying, overwhelming, and opened "new vistas of enterprise and adventure, which he was not slow to perceive" (Frear 203). He became a very successful public speaker, public reader and lecturer "who regarded oratory as a carefully calculated art"... (Shavelenko 147).

The Sandwich Islands lectures became a huge success; and soon he was delivering the same lecture, with some variations, in California towns. Then came the West, Midwest, the East, and England. He stood before his audience as the public personality "Mark Twain," making a striking appearance on stage with his reddish-brown hair, keen eyes, mustache, and slightly awkward carriage; and he was noted for his monotonous drawl and dramatic pauses. He became very much in demand as a lecturer, and lecturing was very lucrative. Hawaii appeared to have given Mark Twain the help he needed at the right time and place in his life. What a publicity agent he became for Hawaii as he admonished his listeners: "If you would see magnificent scenery--scenery on a mighty scale--and get scenery which charms with its softness and delights you with its unspeakable beauty, at the same moment that it deeply impresses you with its grandeur and its sublimity, you should go to the islands" (qtd. in M. Clemens *The Honolulu, Star-Bulletin* 10).

The fifth volume of Thomas B. Reed's *Modern Eloquence* contains a lecture by Mark Twain on the Sandwich Islands. The editor, in an explanatory note, says that the manuscript was not preserved, and that this particular fragment was reprinted from a newspaper of the time. It was one of Mr. Clemens's early lectures and was repeated in many parts of the country, it adding materially to his fame as an American humorist of high degree:

> As I have spent several months in the Islands several years ago, I feel competent to shed any amount of light upon the matter ... Eighty or ninety years ago they had a native population of full four hundred thousand souls and they were comfortable, prosperous and happy. But then the white people came and brought trade, and commerce, and education, and complicated diseases, and civilization, and other calamities, and as a consequence the poor natives began to die off with a wonderful rapidity, so that forty or fifty years ago the 400,000 had become reduced to 200,000. Then the white people doubled the education facilities and

this doubled the death rate ... The Hawaiians are a very gentle, kind-hearted race. They are a very hospitable people indeed--very hospitable. In olden times it used to be popular to call the Sandwich Islanders cannibals, but they were never cannibals. That is amply proven ... The land that I have tried to tell you about lies out there in the midst of the watery wilderness, in the very heart of the limitless solitudes of the Pacific. It is a dreamy, beautiful, charming land. (qtd. in McClellan 10)

The Sandwich Islands lecture circuit encompassed the years 1866-1873, and ran as follows:

1866, October 2, Maguire's Academy of Music

1866, October 11, Metropolitan Theater

1866, October 20, Grass Valley, Hamilton Hall

1866, October 23, Nevada City, The Theater

1866, October 24, Red Dog, Odd Fellows Hall or Log School House

1866, October 25, Marysville Theater

1866, October 25, You Bet, Masonic or Odd Fellows Hall

1866, October 31, Virginia City, Maguire's Opera House

1866, November 3, Carson City, Carson City Theater

1866, November 10, Gold Hill, Gold Hill Theater

1866, November 16, San Francisco, Platt's Hall

1866, November 21, San Jose

1866, November 23, Petaluma

1866, November 27, Oakland, Hall of the College School

1866, December 10, San Francisco, Congress Hall

1867, March 25, St. Louis, Mercantile Library Hall

1867, March 26, St. Louis, Mercantile Library Hall

1867, April 2, Hannibal, Brittingham Hall

1867, April 8, Keokuk, Chatham Square M. E. Church

1867, April 9, Quincy, National Hall

1867, May 6, New York, Cooper Institute

1867, May 10, Brooklyn, Brooklyn Athanaeum

1867, May 15, New York, Irving Hall

1868, February 22, Georgetown, Forrest hall

1869, November 9, Providence, Harrington's Opera House

1869, November 10, Boston, Music Hall

1869, November 23, Hartford, Allyn Hall

1869, December 7, Philadelphia, Academy of Music

1869, December 29, Portland, Mercantile Library Association

1869, January 10, Albany, Twiddle Hall

1873, January 31, Hartford, Allyn Hall

1873, February 5, New York, Steinway Hall

1873, February 7, Brooklyn, Academy of Music

1873, February 10, New York, Steinway Hall

1873, October 13-18, London, Queen's Concert Rooms, Hanover Square

1873, October 20, Liverpool, Liverpool Institute

1873, December 1-2, 3 (twice), 4-6, London, Queen's Concert Rooms, Hanover Square (Frear 421-26)

Frear states that Twain gave his lectures numerous times, and may have given the Sandwich Islands lecture once in Washington in 1867, and once in Philadelphia in 1868. Mark Twain may also have given the lectures at places other than those mentioned during the season of 1869-70, including a lecture to the school children of Carson City (Frear 426).

Mark Twain would give the Sandwich Islands lecture more often than any other, almost one hundred times in the United States and England, usually announcing the title as "Our Fellow Savages of the Sandwich Islands" (Fatout 648-659). The year 1873 was the last year for the lectures on the Sandwich Islands. King Kamehameha V's death on December 11, 1872, had revived interest in the topic. Twain would comment a letter to *The New York Daily Tribune*, January 3, 1873:

> The late King Kamehameha V was a wise sovereign who had seen something of the world; he was educated and

accomplished, and he tried hard to do well by his people and succeeded ... he was popular, greatly respected, and even beloved ... I can imagine what is going on in Honolulu now, during this month of mourning, for I was there when the late King's sister, Victoria, died. (qtd. in Frear 500)

Mark Twain delivered in England later that year, as far as we know in 1873, the last lectures on this topic. *The Standard*, a London newspaper, would comment:

Mark Twain delivered a most amusing lecture last evening on the subject of the Sandwich Islands ... the room was crowded with ladies and gentlemen amongst whom there were many celebrities, musical, dramatic and literary; and one man of world-wide fame entitled to special mention--the great American showman Mr. Barnum. (Frear 445)

The popularity of the lectures was unprecedented. Paine says that Mark Twain was "the most talked of figure in London." In a supplement to *The Liverpool Journal*, October 20, 1873, Mr. Twain was called "the great American humorist" (Frear 445). *The Liverpool Journal* also said:

Mark Twain keeps his audience in uproarious laughter during his lecture ... introducing at times eloquent descriptive pieces of the great volcano and the lovely and languishing picture of the islands ... Mark Twain will be able to make a fortune on his return from America, out of the Sandwich Islands, and will find other topics equally capable of his highly original treatment when that is exhausted. (Frear 446)

He had passed his final tests as lecturer: San Francisco, New York, Boston, and London.

Between December 1866 and August 1869, he had lectured at Cooper Union in New York, visited the Holy Land for the *San Francisco Alta California*, become engaged to his future wife, Olivia Langdon, and conducted a strenuous lecture tour.

One of the first Sandwich Islands speeches given in San Francisco October 2, 1866, contained some of the following comments, compiled in a collection of Mark Twain's lectures by Fatout:

> The first object I ever saw in the Sandwich Islands was a repulsive one. It was a case of Oriental leprosy, of so dreadful a nature that I have never been able to get it out of my mind since ... these islands were discovered some eighty or ninety years ago by Captain Cook ... when these islands were discovered the population was about 400,000, but the white man came and brought various complicated diseases, education and civilization ... Consequently, the population began to drop off with commendable activity. Population soon dwindled down to 200,000, and then down to 55,000, and it is proposed to send a few more missionaries and finish them ... In color, the natives are a rich, dark brown--a sort of black and tan, a very pleasing tint. The native women in the rural districts wear a loose, magnificent curtain calico

> garment ... They are very fond of their dogs. They feed them, pet them, take ever so much care of them, and then cook them and eat them. I couldn't do that. I would rather go hungry for two days than devour an old personal friend that way ... a Kanaka will eat anything he can bite--a live fish, scales and all, which must be rather annoying to the fish ... these Sandwichers believe in a superstition that the biggest liars in the world have got to visit the islands some time before they die ... they have several specimens of liars they boast of. (Fatout 4-14)

The Cooper Union lecture in New York turned out to be most advantageous. Mark Twain's friend, Frank Fuller, suggested to him that he should take the biggest hall in New York and deliver his lecture on the Sandwich Islands. He told Twain that the people would be wild to hear him. Fuller told Twain to leave it to him--that he would lay fame and fortune at his feet. Fuller sent baskets full of complimentary passes to every public-school teacher within a radius of thirty miles of New York. A prospectus of the lecture was distributed in New York, and stated:

> Mark Twain will deliver a serio-humorous lecture concerning Kanakadom or the Sandwich Islands at the Cooper Institute on Monday evening, May 6, 1867. Tickets are fifty cents and are for sale at Checkering and Sons, 652 Broadway, and at principal hotels in New York. Doors open at 7 o'clock. The wisdom will begin to flow at 8 ... the following topics will receive marked attention: how the

> natives dress and how they don't dress, the King, the other natives, native hospitality, native rascality, how they dispose of their dogs, what becomes of the surplus children, the boohoo fever, terrific drinkers, a powerful description of a volcanic eruption ... carefully elaborated jokes will be attached to these subjects, pathos will be infused into this lecture, and people who are overcome by it may go out for a few minutes; but no weeping will be allowed on the premises... (Frear 454-55)

There was even a letter of reference in the prospectus from Mr. James W. Nye, a U. S. Senator and former Nevada Governor, who was to preside over and introduce the lecture. Mr. Nye states:

> I am pleased that you ... are to repeat in New York that excellent lecture on the Sandwich Islands to which I listened to with great interest some months ago in San Francisco. Compromising as your lecture does, an array of facts together with descriptions of life, manners and customs among the natives of the Islands of the Pacific, and embellished as it is with a sparkling wit and genial humor, wholly peculiar and unexcelled, I desire to commend it most warmly, and to express the hope that the intelligent citizens of the metropolis will extend to it and you, the cordial and hearty welcome which both so signally deserve. As a citizen of my own mountain state of Nevada, and one universally, respected, I shall rejoice in your success. (Frear 455)

Charles Neider mentions that Mark Twain said of the event:

> ...when I got near the building I found that all the streets for a quarter of a mile around were blocked with people, and traffic was stopped ... I found my way around to the back of the building and got in there by the stage door. And sure enough the seats, the aisles, the great stage itself was packed with bright looking human beings ... I was happy and I was excited beyond expression. I poured the Sandwich Islands out on to those people with a free hand and they laughed and shouted to my entire content ... Fuller was right about the fame. I certainly did get a working quantity of fame out of that lecture. The New York newspapers praised it. The country newspapers copied those praises ... The lyceums of the country began to call for me ... I had acquired fame and also a fortune. (qtd. in Neider 172)

An article printed in *The New York Tribune* May 11, 1867, gave Twain a very positive review. It stated that Mark Twain had a brilliant reception at the Cooper Institute. "The hall was crowded beyond all expectation ... no other lecturer, of course excepting Artemus Ward, has so thoroughly succeeded in exciting the mirthful curiosity, and compelling the laughter of his hearers"... (Budd 18).

Another famous speech was the April 8, 1889 one presented at Delmonico's in New York. Theodore Roosevelt was there, along with A. G. Spalding, president of the Chicago National League Club. Spalding had financed the globe-circling tour of two teams, the All-Americans and the Chicagos. Mark Twain, shortstop, was introduced as a native of the Sandwich Islands. Fatout gives some of Mark Twain's spoken revelations:

> In those Islands the cats haven't any tales, and the snakes haven't any teeth; and what is still more irregular, the man that loses a game gets the pot. And as to dress: the native women all wear a single garment—but the men don't. No, the men don't wear anything at all, they hate display; when they even wear a smile they think they are overdressed ... speaking of education, everybody there is educated, from the highest to the lowest; in fact, it is the only country in the world where education is actually universal. And yet every now and then you run across instances of ignorance that are simply revolting--simply degrading to the human race. (Fatout 246)

He continues his discourse on the subject of the natives:

> These natives are very hospitable people indeed--very hospitable. If you want to stay a few days and nights in a native's cabin you can stay and welcome. They will do everything they possibly to make you comfortable. They will feed you on baked dog, or poi, or raw fish, or raw salt pork, fricasseed cats--all the luxuries of the season. And if you want to trade, that's quite another matter--that's business! The Kanaka is a born trader. He will swindle you if he can, he will lie straight through from the first word to the last. He will tell gigantic lies that awe you with their grandeur, lies

that stun you with their imperial impossibility ... and as for dying, they can die whenever they want to ... when they take a notion to die they die, and it don't make any difference whether there is anything the matter with them or not. They can't be persuaded out of it. A gentleman in Hawaii asked his servant if he wouldn't like to die and have a big funeral. He said yes, and looked happy. And the next morning the overseer came and said, 'That boy of yours laid down and died last night and said you were going to give him a fine funeral'. (Fatout 9)

Twain continues his speech with comments about Hawaiian funerals:

They are very fond of funerals. Big funerals are their main weakness. Fine grave clothes, fine funeral appointments, and a long procession of things they take a generous delight in. Years ago a Kanaka and his wife were condemned to be hanged for murder. They received the sentence with manifest satisfaction because it gave an opening for a funeral ... it makes but little difference to them whose funeral it is; they would as soon attend their own funeral as anybody else's ... This couple sold every foot of ground they had and laid it out in fine clothes to be hung in. And the woman appeared on the scaffold in a white satin dress and slippers and feathers of gaudy ribbon, and the man was arrayed in a gorgeous vest, blue clawhammer coat and brass buttons, and white kid gloves. As the noose was adjusted around his neck, he blew his nose with a grand theatrical flourish, so as to show his embroidered white handkerchief. I never, never knew of a couple who enjoyed hanging more than they did. (Fatout 9)

The audience was fascinated by his discussion of the Hawaiian's dogs:

> They are very fond of dogs, these people ... they feed their dog, pet him, take ever so much care of him, and then cook and eat him. I couldn't do that. I would rather go hungry for two days than devour an old personal friend in that way ... at this point in my lecture I usually illustrate cannibalism, but I am a stranger here and don't feel like taking liberties ... still, if anyone in the audience will lend me an infant, I will illustrate the matter ... with all these excellent and hospitable ways these Kanakers have some cruel instincts. They will put a live chicken in the fire just to see it hop about ... they would also kill an infant now and then--bury him alive sometimes; but the missionaries have annihilated infanticide--for my part I can't see why. (Fatout 11)

With a prophesy of the future, Twain says: "Now, you see what kind of voters you will have if you take those islands away from these people as we are pretty sure to do some day"
(Fatout 11).

These many versions of the Sandwich Islands lectures evolved from Mark Twain's four month stay on the Hawaiian Islands in 1866, and his twenty-five letters from there published in *The*

Sacramento Union. From this time forward, Mark Twain was caught up by the currents of popularity and swept from one success to another. He had struck his bonanza, not in silver as he had once dreamed in the West, but in his spoken word and by seeing his stories in print. He was quick to realize that the lectures created a 'voice' or personality for 'Mark Twain.' For ever after he used his Missouri drawl both to make his lectures uniquely entertaining and to give his writing a tempo and rhythm that no other humorist could match" (Gerber 21).

By the fall of October 1871, Twain was married and was looking forward to his second book, *Roughing It*, to be published the following February. It would be almost a biographical story of the seven formative years during which he emerged as a writer and stage personality:

> ...evolving into that eventual role from a beginning as a Mississippi River pilot, then as an assistant to his brother in the new Nevada Territorial government, then as a miner, then as a newspaper correspondent and city editor in Virginia City, then on to Sacramento, San Francisco, and Hawaii before conquering the world with his wit and wisdom. (Jones, *Mark Twain in Hawaii* iii)

As his 1871 lecture tour ended, he was hoping for success with *Roughing It*. It was not as successful as *The Innocents Abroad*, but it sold over 72,000 copies in a two year period. He received favorable reviews: "Mark Twain's genius is characterized by the breadth, and ruggedness, and audacity of the West" (Emerson 68). With this second success, Mark Twain appeared to be established at last.

Accounts of domestic and foreign travel comprised a substantial part of Mark Twain's writings. These accounts are in the three major books he wrote on foreign travel--*The Innocents Abroad, A Tramp Abroad*, and *Following the Equator*; two books on domestic travel--*Roughing It* (to which he appended a revised version of his Sandwich Island letters) and *Life on the Mississippi*; and numerous short magazine and newspaper articles (West 13).

The Innocents Abroad was published in 1869 and was based on letters Mark Twain wrote in 1867 to the San Francisco Alta California and *The New York Tribune* and *Herald*, describing the tour of the steamship *Quaker City* to Europe, Egypt, and the Holy Land. *Roughing It,* mentioned earlier, was published in 1872. The book is based on Twain's own experiences during the 1860's, and pulls material from his Sandwich Islands letters. The second part relates portions of the Sandwich Island travel adventure. *A Tramp Abroad*, published in 1880, is a travel narrative about his walking trip through the Black Forest and the Alps. *Life on the Mississippi* was published in 1883. *Following the Equator*, an autobiographical narrative, was published in 1897, and describes Mark Twain's 1895 lecture tour around the world. It has an undercurrent of bitterness not found in his earlier travel books.

Gary West, in *The Mark Twain Journal*, believes that the chief distinction of Mark Twain's travel writing is his "assumption of a clearly defined persona: that of a plain-speaking Western American who makes no pretensions to culture or education" (West 13). West also believes that in Twain's travel writing he insists on a realistic perspective, being eager to expose sham and deception, and being quick to moralize using American standards as his touchstone.

In the Sandwich Islands letters Mark Twain appears to be sentimental and tolerant, but in his later travel writings he becomes more uncultured and thus more able to condemn what he feels is offensive or immoral. The early travel letters are more journalistic than literary, but they do reveal a Mark Twain experimenting with techniques and themes toward the dual purpose of being informative and humorous.

In the years 1866-71 Mark Twain had slowly begun his rise to being the "The People's Author," having left his Bohemian life in the sagebrush. He went East, made his "mark," married into Eastern wealth and status, became a gentleman and a newspaper owner, lived in a brownstone mansion and was driven about in his own carriage by a liveried coachman, thanks to royalties and lecture fees (Leary 18) . He never forgot Burlingame's advice during these years. "Later he liked to tell and retell what his friend William Dean Howells called 'the inexhaustible, the fairy, the Arabian Nights story' of his life. His success would shape the dreams of young authors setting out to conquer America" (Kaplan 67). What started out to be a different attempt to make a living became instead forty years of lectures and reading engagements--and gave the world a literary treat while doing much to add to Mark Twain's immortality. It appeared Hawaii had given Mark Twain the help he needed at a dark time of his life when he needed help most. The turning point was over, thanks to Hawaii, Burlingame, and the lectures.

A "maturing" Mark Twain

CHAPTER FOUR

THE HAWAII NOVEL

"Mark Twain's failure to produce a Hawaii novel which he nourished in his imagination for nearly half a century was a literary misfortune for Hawaii" (Horton 96). It would appear that Mark Twain procrastinated too long on Hawaii as the theme of fiction. As mentioned earlier, there was no formal book publication of the *Sandwich Island Letters* until 1937, years after his death in 1910. George Wharton James, writing in *The Pacific Monthly* in 1910, would blame the publishing life and timing, and the publication of Charles Warren Stoddard's *South Sea Idylls*:

> It is a singular thing that Mark Twain's great friend, Charles Warren Stoddard, and Twain should both have been sent to the Sandwich Islands in the early part of their careers, and I am under the impression that if Stoddard had never published his *South Sea Idylls*, Mark Twain's correspondence from the Islands would have been edited and put in a book long ago. (Horton 97)

Mark Twain: Later Years

Perhaps it was not easy in 1866 to sell the New York publishers on a book about the Hawaiian Islands. A few months after his return from the Hawaiian Islands Mark Twain was talking of getting "an illustrated book on the Sandwich Islands" but felt it would not be accepted by his New York publishers, Dick & Fitzgerald (Horton 97). In 1870 he wrote to A. F. Judd, later a Chief Justice of Hawaii, that he still wanted to do a book about the Islands.

Frear believes that the real reason that the Hawaii book was not written was that it was crowded out by the rush and press of other matters--lectures, travels, other correspondence, books, etc.--so fast did things pile up on him after his Sandwich Islands visit (Frear 234). Mark Twain did continue to add bits and pieces to his Hawaii story idea, some written and some spoken as a lecturer. One such story, "My Platonic Sweetheart," was written about a particular dream he had about Hawaii. The story was rejected by a magazine and not published until two years after his death. The setting was the Iao Valley on Maui. Frear includes portions of this story in Appendix K. The story originally appeared in *Harper's Magazine*, December, 1912. Mark Twain mentions a strange, recurring dream that sometimes even overtook him in the midst of his lectures:

> Soon that familiar dream-voice spoke my name, and swept all my troubles away ... she called me Robert, and I called her Agnes. The next moment we two were lounging up the blossomy gorge called the Iao Valley in the Hawaiian Islands. I recognized, without any explanations, that Robert was not my name, but only a pet name, a common noun, and it meant 'dear.' Both of us knew that Agnes was not a name, but only a pet name, a common noun, whose spirit was affectionate, but not conveyable with exactness in any but the dream-language ... in one of my notebooks there are several letters from this dream-sweetheart, in some unknown tongue--with translations added. She says, 'Rax oha tal,' and I translate that as 'when you receive this it will remind you that I long to see your face and touch your hand, for the comfort of it and the peace.' We wandered far up the fairy

gorge, gathering the beautiful flowers of the ginger-plant and talking affectionate things, and tying and retying each other's ribbons and cravats, which didn't need it; and finally sat down in the shade of a tree and climbed the vine-hung precipices with our eyes, up and down toward the sky to where the drifting scarves of white mist clove them across and left green summits floating pale and remote, like spectral islands wandering in the deeps of space; and then we descended to earth and talked again. (Frear 481)

Then a fascinating conversation occurs between Robert and Agnes. Robert asks Agnes if she has ever been in the region before and she replies: "Once, but it wasn't an island then ... it was a sufa" (quoted in Frear 481). Twain remarks that he understood that she meant the islands were at that time part of a continent. Agnes further states that there were no people there then, and that she travels a great deal in the stars. "You will go with me sometime, Robert, and you will see" (Frear 481).

Other published writings based on his Sandwich Islands trip included "Remarkable Instances of Presence of Mind" (about the *Ajax*'s first voyage to Hawaii), and "A Strange Dream." The former is about the *Ajax*'s first voyage to Hawaii, and the latter based upon the search for Kamehameha's bones at the Kilauea Volcano (Horton 98).

Frear reprints portions of a "A Strange Dream," in Appendix B, from *The New York Saturday Press*, June 2, 1866. One of the most interesting parts follows:

After I had gone to bed, I got to thinking of the volcanic magnificence we had witnessed, and could not go to sleep. I hunted up a book and concluded to pass the time in reading. The first chapter I came upon related several instances of remarkable revelations, made to men through the agency of dreams--of roads and houses, trees, fences and all manner of landmarks, shown in visions and recognized afterwards in waking hours, and which served to point the way to some dark mystery or other. (Frear 253)

Mark Twain dreamed that he was in the bowels of the earth, in the presence of death! He dreamed he saw the crumbling skeleton of King Kamehameha the Great:

I woke up. How glad I was to know it was all a dream ... so I turned over, fell asleep, and dreamed the same dream precisely as before ... I woke up and reflected long upon the curious and singularly vivid dream ... I fell asleep and again dreamed the same dream ... I could not sleep and waited for daylight, and descended to the wide plain in the crater. (Frear 254)

Mark Twain decided that this was no dream, but a revelation from the supernatural.

He labored several hours to remove the huge stone he had seen in his dream. The mysterious boulder would not budge, but Twain believed that it was covering the King's grave:

> Hour after hour I labored, growing more and more weary, but still upheld by a fascination which I felt was infused into me by the invisible powers whose will I was working. At last I concentrated my strength in a final effort, and the stone rolled from its position ... there were no bones there. And I said to myself, 'well, if this ain't the blastedest infernalest hum-bug that ever I've come across yet, I wish I may never' ... you cannot bet anything on dreams. (Frear 255)

According to Horton, only pieces of the Hawaii story remain. Mark Twain had a theme; he had a central character, but he never finished the story (Horton 98). Eighteen years after he had been in Hawaii, 1884, his literary fame was well in place. He wrote to his friend, W.D. Howells, telling him that he had saturated himself with knowledge of an unimaginably beautiful land that had the most strange and fascinating people. He had begun a story:

> My billiard table is stacked up with books relating to the Sandwich Islands; the walls are upholstered with scraps of paper penciled with notes drawn from them. The story's hidden motive will illustrate a but-little considered fact in human nature; that the religious folly you are born in you will die in, no matter what apparently reasonable religious folly may seem to have taken its place meanwhile, and abolished and obliterated it... (Horton 98)

Mark Twain continues:

I start with Bill Ragsdale at 12 years of age, and the heroine at 4, in the midst of the ancient idolatrous system, with its picturesque and amazing customs and superstitions, 3 months before the arrival of the missionaries and the erection of a shallow Christianity upon the ruins of the old paganism. Then these two will become educated Christians, and highly civilized ... then I will jump fifteen years, and do Bill Ragsdale's leper business. When we come to dramatize, we can draw a great deal of matter from the story, all ready to our hand. (qtd. in Day, *Letters* 25)

Grove Day mentions that in his study of Paine's collection of *Twain's Letters*, Paine says that the author never finished the story, but in the letters of January 24 and 30, 1884, to Twain's friend Mrs. Fairbanks, Twain said he had finished it and was about to give it a painstaking revision. In a letter of February 25 of the same year, Mark Twain asked Howells if he had yet blocked out the Sandwich Islands play--as if he had sent the story to Howells for the purpose of making it into a drama (Day 26).

In the Mark Twain Collection at the University of California Library at Berkeley one can view seventeen pages of a manuscript of this novel, of which nine pages contain an ornate description of the islands. There is a brief section consisting of a dialogue between a king and a boy whose sister has been threatened with death, but is released. A third fragment mentions a king's stolen spittoon (Day 26).

The selection below is from the opening of the novel's rough draft and is reminiscent of Mark Twain's later famous prose poem:

> The date is 1840. Scene the true isles of the Blest; that is to say, the Sandwich Islands--to this day the peacefullest, restfullest, sunniest, balmiest, dreamiest haven of refuge for a worn and weary spirit the surface of the earth can offer. Away out there in the mid-solitudes of the vast Pacific, and far down to the edge of the tropics, they lie asleep on the waves, perpetually green and beautiful, remote from the work-day world and its frets and worries, a bloomy fragrant paradise, where the troubled may go and find peace, and the sick and tired find strength and rest. There they lie, the divine islands, forever shining in the sun, forever smiling out on the sparkling sea, with its soft mottlings of drifting cloud-shadows and vagrant cat's-paws of wind; forever inviting you, never repulsing you; and whosoever looks upon them once will never more get the picture out of his memory till he die. With him it will stay, and be always present; always present and always fresh; neither time nor distance can dim its features, or dull their charm, or reconcile him to the thought that he will never see that picture with his eyes of flesh again. (qtd. in Day, *Letters* 27)

At any rate, there is no known fictional book about Hawaii explicitly by Mark Twain, with the exception of the chapters about his Sandwich Islands experiences in the second half of *Roughing It*. These chapters are composed of about one-third of the subject matter covered by the letters to the *Union* with additional new materials written (Frear 235). These chapters used thirty thousand words from the letters and added some five thousand words of new material. This shorter, later version of Mark Twain's Hawaiian adventures is smoothly written and artfully told. A good example of this style is found in Mark Twain's passage about explorations in the volcano region. He writes the following about Haleakala Crater at sunrise:

> It had a growing warmth around it suffusing the horizon. Soon the sun emerged and looked out over the cloud-waste, flinging bars of ruddy light across it; staining its folds and billow-caps with blushes, purpling the shaded troughs between, and glorifying the massy vapor-palaces and cathedrals with a wasteful splendor of all blendings and combinations of rich coloring. (*Roughing It* 84)

Perhaps the reason that the Hawaii story was never written was that it was a victim of circumstance, but Grove Day cites scholars who believe the Hawaii novel came to form in *A Connecticut Yankee in King Arthur's Court*, a realistic-satirical fantasy of kings and knights. The main character, transposed back into an earlier time in a time machine, attempts to change a civilization according to the governing rules of his century. Day further believes that Professor Fred W. Lorch's article in *American Literature* in March, 1958, "attempts to show that many of the basic concepts of feudal society and its practices which come under attack in *Yankee* had their inception from Mark Twain's early observations of life in the

Sandwich Islands, and particularly in his wide reading of the history of the Sandwich Islands" (Day 27). Mark Twain had supposedly read James Jackson Jarves' *History of the Hawaiian Islands*, a book which he had "borrowed" from the library of Father Damon's Mission in Honolulu and taken away without permission (Day, *Letters* 22). From this reading he served his indictment of social, political, and religious practices in *Yankee*. Lorch believed that Twain's use of the tabu system by the Hawaiian priests could be compared to Jarves' writing about the interdict of the Church of Rome and in the *Yankee* novel the dread interdict defeats "The Boss's" Republican plans. Says Lorch: "No less remarkable is the similar between the role of the American missionaries who destroyed the old order in the Sandwich Islands and the role of the Connecticut Yankee who sought to free King Arthur's serfs in much the same way (Day 28).

The Lorch article also attempted to show that "to an important degree the *Yankee* sprang out of the tale of a Sandwich Islands novel Mark Twain was busily at work on in the spring of 1883-84, immediately prior to the time he came upon Mallory's *Morte d' Arthur*" (Lorch). On the evidence of Twain's letters to Howells and Mrs. Fairbanks, the manuscript fragments in Berkeley, and the author's remarks here and there about Bill Ragsdale, we perhaps could deduce that Hank Morgan in *Yankee* was a characterization of Ragsdale.

Hank Morgan appears to be a missionary of modern theories about society, much like the missionaries who traveled to Hawaii in the 1800's. Before the final battle in *Yankee,* Morgan's right-hand man selects an elite squadron of boys from fourteen to seventeen who hopefully would not have been inundated with priestly superstitions, typical of the Hawaiian youths. Even Merlin seems to bear a resemblance to the sorcerer in ancient Hawaiian legends.

The inconstancy and incontinence of the women in the court in *Yankee* reflect observations of early Hawaiian visitors about maidens eager to offer their charms to any male. Lorch also feels that there was a parallel between King Arthur and King Kamehameha V. After all, the Hawaiian king was the first reigning monarch that Mark Twain ever knew.

Mark Twain, in the preface to *Yankee,* mentions that there are customs touched upon in the story that are historical, even mentioning that the laws and customs written about could have existed in civilizations of far later times. He also mentions discussing the divine right of kings, and the merits of an ideal king: one of lofty character and extraordinary ability (Twain, *Unabridged* 959).

Critics were surprised that Mark Twain was able to deliver the manuscript to *A Connecticut Yankee in King Arthur's Court* in a short time. Perhaps the reason, as Lorch believes, was because Twain incorporated these ideas about a Hawaiian novel into the satirical *Yankee.*

The final scene in this bittersweet saga is Mark Twain's return to Paradise. Like the many millions of tourists who had come before him and would come after, he had vowed to return. Seven years after his visit there he had said in a letter written for *The New York Tribune,* "If I could have my way about it, I would go back there and remain the rest of my days" (Horton 99). Later, in 1881, Mark Twain wrote to Charles Warren Stoddard, in the midst of carpenters and decorators in his home:

> If only the house would burn down, we could pack up the cubs and fly to the isles of the blest, and shut ourselves up in the healing solitudes of Haleakala and get a good rest; for the mails do not intrude there, nor yet the telephone and the telegraph ... Maybe you think that I am not happy: the very thing that gravels me is that I am. I don't want to be happy when I can't work: I am resolved that hereafter I won't be. What I have always longed for was the privilege of living forever away up on one of those mountains in the Sandwich Islands overlooking the sea. (qtd. in Horton79)

In 1895, after 29 long years of dreaming about Hawaii, Mark Twain prepared to return there. He would be making a lucrative salary with the hopes of paying off debts of $100,000 due to business disasters, including his own printing machine invention scheme. He had also had bad management by his publishers (Horton 179). The return trip to the Sandwich Islands would be part of a world lecture and reading tour to diminish this debt. To this end, and suffering from carbuncles, bronchitis and rheumatism, and now loathing the lecture business, he set forth in the intense heat of summer on a year's world lecture tour. The trip would be circumstance. It would be an appointment with dreams of youth.

The Charismatic Twain

CHAPTER FIVE

HAWIAII AWAITS A LEGEND
DON'T PART WITH DREAMS OF YOUTH

Mark Twain had indeed come a long way from his first trip in 1866 to Hawaii. Back then he was a young, scrambling reporter for a California newspaper. As his life progressed, he developed a drive for financial success. He had gone through disastrous business endeavors, including the bankruptcy. By 1895 Twain was back with the American Publishing of Hartford traveling around the world to pay off the $100,000 debt, and had started "to write himself into affluence" (Wilson 7). His books were now more complicated and became valuable pieces of merchandise. As he aged, he seemed to ponder about his illusions of life.

Mark Twain had often attempted to look at life through a veil of illusions. In *Following the Equator*, he warned his readers: "Don't part with your illusions. When they are gone, you may still exist, but you have ceased to live" (Bellamy 222). He would remark: "Ah, the dreams of our youth, how beautiful they are, and how perishable! ... Oh, our lost Youth--God keep its memory green in our hearts! For age is upon us, with the indignity of its infirmities, and Death beckons!" (qtd. in Budd, *Speeches* 450). He also wrote in "Old Age" that one needs to climb to a summit in their old age and look back: Ah, then you see!" (qtd. in Budd 719). He commented further:

> Down that far-reaching perspective you can make out each country and climate that you crossed ... you can make out where Infancy merged into Boyhood; Boyhood into down-lipped Youth; Youth into indefinite Young-Manhood; indefinite Young Manhood into definite Manhood; definite Manhood with aggressive ambitions into sobered and heedful Husbandhood and Fatherhood; these into Old Age, white-headed, the temple empty, the idols broken, the worshippers in their graves, nothing left but You, a remnant, a tradition, belated fag-end of a foolish dream, a dream so ingeniously dreamed that it seemed real all the time... (qtd. in Budd 719)

The dream of the Sandwich Islands did call him back and sentiment took hold of him as his ship, the *Warimoo*, steamed to within sight of Diamond Head and Mark Twain encountered the vision of paradise he had longed all those years to see:

> On the seventh day out we saw a dim vast bulk standing up out of the wastes of the Pacific and knew that spectral promontory was Diamond Head, a piece of this world which I had not seen before for 29 years. So we were nearing Honolulu, the capital city of the Sandwich Islands--those islands which to me were paradise; a paradise which I had

been longing all those years to see again. Not any other thing in the world could have stirred me as the sight of that rock did... (Twain, *Following the Equator* 24)

Mildred Clemens would further quote Mr. Twain:

> Many memories of my former visit to the island came up in my mind while we lay at anchor in front of Honolulu that night. And pictures--pictures--pictures--an enchanting procession of them ... we lay in luminous blue water; shoreward the water was green--green and brilliant; at the shore itself it broke in a long white ruffle, and with no crash, no sound that we could hear. The town was buried under a mat of foliage that looked like a cushion of moss. The silky mountains were clothed in soft, rich splendors of melting color, and some of the cliffs were veiled in slanting mists. I recognized it all. It was just as I had seen it long before, with nothing of its beauty lost, nothing of its charm wanting ... and it made one drunk with delight to look upon it. (qtd. in M. Clemens 11)

Mark Twain was scheduled to have lectured in Honolulu. In his notebook he commented on the five hundred booked lecture seats sold out for his advertised appearance. Mark Twain was a legendary writer and performer by 1895, and it was natural that the Hawaiian people were excited that he was coming to the islands. He had made no secret that he had to lecture around-the-world for the honor of discharging the burden of bankruptcy. Twain was eager to return to a land that had offered him the opportunities to make his name known to a wider audience, first as a reporter for his 1866 *Hornet* scoop, and then as a lecturer with his popular "Sandwich Islands" lectures.

Twain and the Customary White Suit

Hawaii prepared for his return trip with much fanfare. Tickets sold fast at the Park Pavilion for the August 24 event (Zmijewski 22). Twain would have only a day in Honolulu due to the tight schedule of the cargo ship *Warrimoo*. Local newspapers informed the public:

> The sale of seats for the Mark Twain lecture on Saturday night has exceeded all expectations, and the success of the affair is already assured. Manager Levey has secured the services of the Kawaihau Quintette Club which will render entirely new selections and songs between the remarks of the humorist ... extra cars will be run on King and Beretania streets before and after the lecture. (Zmijewski 22)

The Independent said: "It is safe to say that every chair which Level can manage to squeeze into the hall will be occupied. It is the one chance in a lifetime to see and hear the greatest humorist of the century" (17 August 3). *The Pacific Commercial Advertiser* said: As a humorist, Mr. Clemens has no equal, and everyone who has read his *Innocents Abroad* or *Tom Sawyer* will enjoy his entertainment and be well repaid for the time and money spent" (21 August, 1).

One more publicity release about Twain came from *The Hawaiian Star* on the day the performance was to be held at Independence Park. The paper printed Twain's own words of praise for the islands, his prose poem.

Twain's visit, which had been advertised for August 24, had to be delayed for a week because the steamer *Warrimoo* had run aground in dense fog soon after leaving Victoria. On the evening of August 30 the *Warrimoo* arrived and anchored off Honolulu. Twain would record in his notebook:

> Oahu ... just as silky and velvety and lovely as ever. If I might, I would go ashore and never leave. The mountains right and left clothed in rich splendor of melting color, fused together. Some of the near cliffs veiled in slanting mists-- beautiful blue water; inshore brilliant green water ... Two sharks playing around laying for a Christian. (qtd. in Wilson 11)

Morning came and with it a tragedy, perhaps a tragedy too melodramatic to be realistic. There had been a plague of cholera in Honolulu, and no one was allowed to leave the ship. One might picture the sight of Mark Twain, standing alone on the deck of the *Warrimoo*, looking toward the Honolulu shore. Perhaps he wondered how the city of Honolulu had changed in twenty-nine years. Later, remembering this moment in *Following the Equator*, he wrote:

> Many memories came up in my mind while we lay at anchor in front of Honolulu that night ... disappointment of course. Cholera had broken out in the town, and we were not allowed to have any communication with the shore. Thus suddenly did my dream of twenty-nine years go to ruin."
> (Twain, *Following the Equator* 31)

Mr. Clarence L. Crabbe remembered the moment well. He was wharf superintendent, and had gone out to the *Warrimoo*. He had immediately recognized Mark Twain, who was reclining on the steamer in a chair with his cap pulled down over his eyes, "looking dreamily up Nuuanu Valley back of 'the white town of Honolulu'" (M. Clemens, "Twain in Paradise" 11). Mr. Crabbe addressed him with the question: "Would you like to go ashore, Mr. Clemens?" To this the reply was, "I would give a thousand dollars to go ashore and not have to return again" (qtd. in M. Clemens, *Honolulu Star Bulletin* 11). Twain said: "Pele's curse had come true after all. She had bested me in the end. Those dreams of my younger days were gone forever" (qtd. in Davids 5).

The *Warrimoo* lay at anchor until midnight that long ago day, and then it bore Mark Twain away forever from the shores of a land he had so longed to return to, but would never physically approach again although he did visit the Hawaiian Islands through his treasured memories and by his writer's pen.

Perhaps it was better this way. Perhaps it was circumstance. Mark Twain was no longer thirty and in reckless pursuit of his destiny. He was famous. He had suffered deep personal tragedies, including the death of his son, Langdon. He had lived in Europe five years and had gone through traumatic business financial losses (Baldanza viii-ix). And the Islands had changed too since their discovery by the civilized world. The Hawaiian Islands he remembered from twenty-nine years ago were an illusion. He mentions in *Following the Equator* that he talked with passengers whose home was Honolulu:

> In my time Honolulu was a beautiful little town, made up of snow-white wooden cottages deliciously smothered in tropical vines and flowers and trees and shrubs; and its coral

roads and streets were hard and smooth, and as white as the houses. The outside aspects of the place suggested the presence of a modest and comfortable prosperity--a general prosperity-- perhaps one might strengthen the term and say universal. There were no fine houses, no fine furniture ... but Mrs. Krout (a passenger on the boat and a current Honolulu resident) said Honolulu had grown wealthy since then, and of course wealth introduced changes; some of the old simplicities have disappeared ... including the riding horse. In Honolulu a few years from now he will be only a tradition... (Twain, *Equator* 33-9)

Better that Mark Twain remember the illusion of his Hawaii as it was when he was young, a wise-cracking, wild spirit with tousled red hair and a mustache, when he was a cigar smoking wanderlust traveler going everywhere, talking to everyone, seeing everything he could see.

Mark Twain would further expound upon the topic in a source some critics consider to be his legendary lost Hawaiian journal:

I certainly must have been daft when I departed from Honolulu in 1866, never to return for 29 years. I probably should have stayed there forever. Literary success has been gratifying, but financial disaster has not. *Tom Sawyer*, *Huckleberry Finn*, *A Connecticut Yankee In King Arthur's Court* and all my other efforts at yarn-spinning may have made me famous, but somehow my pile of debts has always remained higher than my stack of letters from well-wishers and admirers. The fact is, I did not know how well off I was, as a youngster of 30, to have been gallivanting around Honolulu and all those Sandwich Islands. (qtd. in Davids 4)

Many critics believe Mark Twain was one of America's greatest writers, but nothing he would say about Hawaii would be remembered as much as his famous prose poem he wrote and delivered at Delmonico's in New York on April 8, 1889, at a dinner honoring two touring American baseball teams that had stopped briefly in Honolulu. By that time, he was so identified with Hawaii that the master of ceremonies introduced him as a native of the Sandwich Islands. His famous Hawaiian prose poem had now been published in newspapers, periodicals and books all over the world. The poem had been put into verse and set to music, and even printed on a postcard. The October, 1908 issue of *Paradise of the Pacific* would say: "The (prose poem) tribute has been given the widest publicity for the invitation of Hawaii tourist travel hitherward, and no doubt has benefited the Hawaiian Islands in a way its author did not dream of" (McClellan 21: 10-1). The prose poem reads:

> No alien land in all the world has any deep, strong charm for me but that one, no other land could so longingly and so beseechingly haunt me sleeping and waking, through half a lifetime, as that one has done. Other things leave me, but it abides; other things change, but it remains the same. For me its balmy airs are always blowing, its summer seas flashing in the sun, the pulsing of its surf-beat is in my ear; I can see its garlanded crags, its leaping cascades, its plumy palms

drowsing by the shore, its remote summits floating like islands above the cloud rack; I can feel the spirit of its woodland solitudes. I can hear the plash of its brooks; in my nostrils still lives the breath of flowers that perished twenty years ago. (qtd. in Frear 217)

Some journeys with appointments of dreams took Mark Twain away from it all, to places no one knew; some took Mark Twain to where it seemed he had always been. But whether he returned to a new town or visited a new culture, travel to the Hawaiian Islands, for Mark Twain, forever changed the boundaries of the world he once knew. How strange that he could never fully return, and how strange that Hawaii would never leave him. Perhaps it was circumstance.

CONCLUSION

THE FINAL ALOHA

Two years before his death, on Mark Twain's seventy-third birthday, he received a beautiful koa mantel piece from the Hawaiian Promotion Committee. The hard curly koa wood had columns that bore carvings depicting plants and flowers of hau, ilima, taro and fern, with letters in the panel that said Aloha. He also received a breadfruit plaque for mounting above the koa mantelpiece. At that time he was building his new home in Redding, Connecticut, which he called Stormfield. In grateful response he wrote the following letter to a Mr. Wood, the then secretary of the committee:

> The beautiful mantel was put in its place an hour ago, its friendly 'Aloha' was the first uttered greeting my seventy-third birthday received. It is rich in color, rich in quality, and rich in decoration, therefore it exactly harmonizes with the taste for such things I have seldom been able to indulge to my content. It will be a great pleasure to me, daily renewed, to have under my eye this lovely reminder of the loveliest fleet of islands that lies anchored in any ocean, and I beg to

thank the committee for providing me that pleasure. (qtd. in M. Clemens 11)

Mark Twain's trip to the Hawaiian Islands in 1866 was instrumental in launching him as an international writer and lecturer. He wrote of the experience:

> I went to the Sandwich Islands and corresponded thence for *The* Sacramento Union five or six months; in October, 1866, I broke out as a lecturer, and from that day to this I have always been able to gain my living without doing any work; for the writing of books and magazine matter was always play, not work. I enjoyed it; it was merely billiards to me. (qtd. in Neider 29)

The trip to the Hawaiian Islands and the Hawaiian letters have received high praise from critics (Branch 178). They believe that in these letters Mark Twain first "found himself" (Branch 178). It is said that the letters represented his "last fling" as a wild humorist of the old west, and that the letters marked the transition from Sam Clemens, itinerant journalist, to Mark Twain the writer (Branch 178). The letters have been described as his first sustained writing. They have been admired as "excellent reporting, comprehensive and skillful in evoking the geography and culture of the islands. They have been esteemed for a youthful, idyllic tone, eloquent descriptions, an increasingly rich humor, and forceful satire" (Branch 178).

The letters provide a glimpse of a fresh, challenging environment stimulated with good reporting. There is spontaneous saturation in new scenes and people. This leaves the reader with an impression of youth and enthusiasm. The form of the letters permitted Mark Twain to experiment in the narrative, the dramatic incident, and character portrayal.

The *Sandwich Islands Letters* were a vital link in his literary career. They first marked out the characteristic form of his travel books, especially *The Innocents Abroad*, and were the basis for a considerable portion of *Roughing It*. The letters also helped make him one of the best know personalities on the Pacific Coast, and provided him an opportunity for the subject matter for his first of many lecture tours (Branch 180). The trip allowed him to meet and be greatly influenced by a mentor, Anson Burlingame. Some critics believe the trip later was rewritten as the basis for *Connecticut Yankee in King Arthur's Court*. The letters serve as a valuable index to Mark Twain's literary development. The Hawaiian experiences affected the quality of his though and shaped his literary expression:

> They illuminate mental processes that were a lifelong precondition of his polemics, satire, and fiction. More specifically, they clarify the habitual dependence of his thinking upon emotionally tinged concepts of justice and equality, enterprise and progress ... elements that permeate the bulk of his writing. They not only animate his satire and polemics but also are germane to his understanding of character in fiction ... the Hawaiian letters help us to

understand that Mark Twain became increasingly aware of the wide gulf between public and private virtue. Far-reaching social consequences depended upon the good man becoming the good citizen ... his concept of tolerance became broader and more firmly based in realities. (Branch 181- 82)

Mark Twain's observations of the missionaries in Hawaii affected his later thinking on religious issues, namely that the church might serve as a hindrance to progress and be an enemy of human rights. He began to develop somewhat of a pessimistic insight into the nature of the individual, and in his later years developed "generalized empirical judgments of human conduct that covered the nature of man and cosmos, morality and necessity" (Branch 184).

Twain's travels to Hawaii and his letters began this understanding process of mankind. He did want a better world in the here and now. "Between *The Adventures of Huckleberry Finn* and *The Mysterious Stranger* came a deeper understanding of tragic necessity, but Mark Twain continued to prize human affection, generosity, and nobility above all else" (Branch 184).

Mark Twain's return trip to Hawaii was truly an appointment with his dreams. The lure of the Hawaii Islands was held in Mark Twain's memory until his death in 1910. He would comment: "I was young in those days, exceedingly young, marvelously young, younger than I am now, younger than I shall ever be again, by hundreds of years" (*Autobiography I*, 245).

Mark Twain wrote about old age in his poem, "To the Above Old People." The poem was written September 15, 1899, from Sanna, Sweden. He had gone there in hopes that there would be a cure for his older daughter, Jean, who had epilepsy. The poem was printed in January, 1900, along with an article titled: "My Boyhood Dreams":

> While yet the Phantom of false Youth was mine,
>
> I heard a Voice from out the Darkness whine,
>
> 'O Youth, O whither gone? Return,
>
> And bathe my Age in thy reviving Wine'
> . . . .
> O Voices of the Long Ago that were so dear!
>
> Fall'n Silent, now, for many a Mould'ring Year,
>
> O Whither are ye flown? Come back
>
> And break my Heart, but bless my grieving ear.
> . . . .
> So let me grateful drain the Magic Bowl
>
> That medicines hurt Minds and on the Soul
>
> The Healing of its Peace doth lay--if then
>
> Death claim me--Welcome be his Dole!

Riverboats, Hannibal, Mississippi, Missouri, *Life on the Mississippi*, *Tom Sawyer* and *Huckleberry Finn*, *The Prince and the Pauper*, *A Connecticut Yankee in King Arthur's Court*, *Roughing It*,

Following the Equator: these are some of the topics and works of Mark Twain best known to the average reader. Most readers also know that the older Mark Twain wore white suits to match his white hair and white shaggy mustache. Most know that Mark Twain was not his real name; he was Samuel Clemens instead. But how many readers know that the Sandwich Islands trip was the catapulting event that would fire Mark Twain to the ascension of literary greatness? Rudyard Kipling called Mark Twain "beyond question the largest man of his time" (Horton 88). William Dean Howells declared: "Emerson, Longfellow, Lowell, Holmes--I knew them all and all the rest of our sages, poets, seers, critics, humorists; they were like one another and like other literary men; but Clemens was sole, incomparable, the Lincoln of our literature (Howells 101).

Rudyard Kipling said, "To my mind Mark Twain was beyond question the largest man of his time, both in the direct outcome of his work and more important still, if possible, in his indirect influence as a protesting force in an age of iron philistinism" (Frear vii).

In a letter to George Ade, June 2, 1941 on the occasion of the founding of the Mark Twain Association of America, Stephen Leacock reiterated the praise of Kipling and Howells:

> I have always looked on Mark Twain as the greatest literary figure that America has seen, and the most truly American ... more than that, I think that Mark Twain, by the spirit that animates all his books--his hatred of tyranny and injustice, his sympathy with the oppressed individual, did more than

any other writer towards making the idea of liberty a part of the American heritage. (Leacock, *The Twainian* 10)

This historical non-fiction book, *Mark Twain's Visits to the Sandwich Islands-An Appointment With Dreams*, has examined Mark Twain's two visits to Hawaii, his memoirs of those visits, the impact of the Hawaiian memories of people and legends on his writing and speaking, and the career elevating letters about the experience written for *The Union*. It has also examined his Sandwich Islands lectures. As Mark Twain shared his regard for Hawaii with his audiences in verbal and written form, he was catapulted into fame and fortune. His enjoyment of the islands was enhanced by his finding himself a celebrity, revered by American and international audiences (Long and Master 71-72). He became one of the most sought after American public speakers. The combination of the Sandwich Island letters to the *Union* and the lectures led directly to his excursion in *The Innocents Abroad,* and gave him, after his lengthy period of unsophisticated apprenticeship in the West, a good start on his phenomenal world career as speaker, writer, and personality. Those four months in the Sandwich Islands in 1866 as correspondent for the *Union* would lead him back to San Francisco, delivering the first lecture, and then on to New York as roving correspondent.

In 1869 *The Innocents Abroad* would be published. In 1870 he would marry Olivia Langdon, and then release *Roughing It* in 1872. The rest is literary history. He would become the first great American writer who was also a popular writer. From the Sandwich

Islands trip in 1866, he had an oasis of a golden memory. He had made the transition from cruder, earlier writings to more refined form, and had a new, lucrative profession: lecturer. In contrast to the 30-year-old young man who had left San Francisco for Honolulu in 1866, Mark Twain's appointment with dreams had turned him into an internationally respected writer, lecturer, and personality.

Throughout his long life (he died in 1910 at the age of seventy-five), Mark Twain would often publish his observations on travel, and many times mentioned the dream motif, but perhaps the most poignant and spiritually revealing is the recounting of his dream of the beautiful maiden on Maui and the effect her demise had upon him. For a man who was born living on our earthly plane and his thoughts of his youth and progression of mental growth as he aged can best be summed up with the following passage on the privilege of man to dream:

> For everything in a dream is more deep and strong and sharp and real than is ever its pale imitation in the unreal life which is ours when we go about awake and clothed with our artificial selves in this vague and dull-tinted artificial world. When we die we shall slough off this cheap intellect, perhaps, and go abroad into Dreamland clothed in our real selves, and aggrandized and enriched by the command over the mysterious mental magician who is here not our slave, but only our guest. ("Platonic Sweetheart," *Harper's Magazine*, December 1912)

In 1910 Mark Twain spent January to April 12 in Bermuda. He had been having frequent, severe chest pains and left for home. He died at his estate, Stormfield, at approximately 6:30 p.m. on April 21, and was buried next to his wife and three children at a family plot in Elmira, New York. "As he had foretold, the return of the mysterious visitor from beyond the solar system under whose sign he had been born, Halley's Comet, returned" (DeVoto 25). Mark Twain had experienced the romantic lure of the islands and the opportunity his first visit there as a young man gave him: an opportunity to catapult into fame and fortune. Mark Twain had truly kept his appointment with dreams.

"I came in with Halley's Comet in 1835 and I expect to go out with it (in 1910)"
- Mark Twain (b.1835 - d.1910)

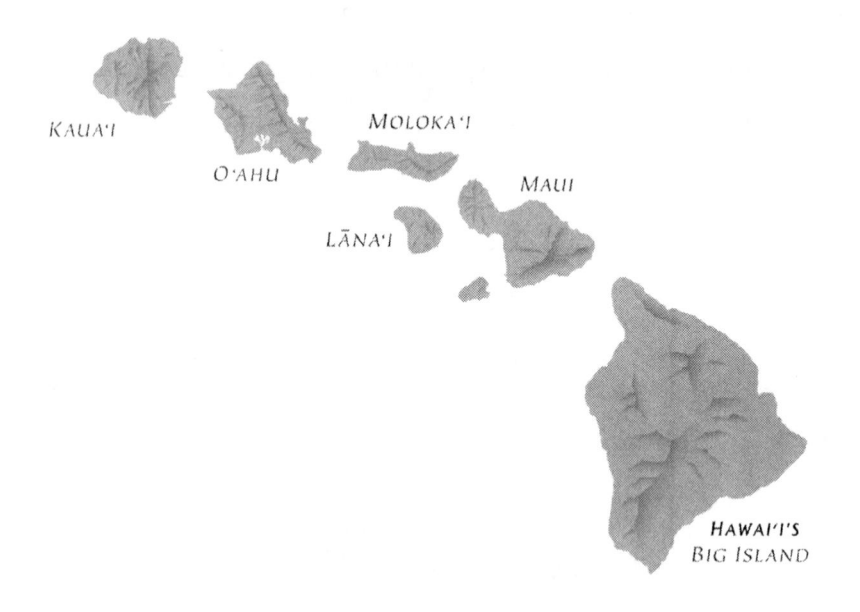

The blessed Sandwich Islands

WORKS CITED

Abramson, Joan. Introduction. *Volume I-Letters From the Sandwich Islands*. By Mark Twain. Norfork, Australia: Island Heritage Ltd., 1975.

Baldanza, Frank. *Mark Twain: An Introduction and Interpretation*. New York: Barnes and Noble, 1961.

Bellamy, Gladys Carmen. *Mark Twain as a Literary Artist*. Norman: U of Oklahoma P, 1950.

Branch, Edgar Marquess. *The Literary Apprenticeship of Mark Twain*. Urbana: U of Illinois P, 1950.

Budd, Louis J. *Critical Essays on Mark Twain, 1867-1910*. Boston: G. K. Hall, 1982.

Budd, Louis J. *Collected Tales, Sketches, Speeches & Essays 1891-1910*. New York: Literary Classics of the US, 1992.

Clemens, Mildred. "Mark Twain in Paradise." *The Honolulu Star Bulletin* 7 Dec. 1935: 9.

---. "Mark Twain in Paradise." *The Honolulu Star Bulletin* 31 Dec. 1935: 8.

---. "Trailing Mark Twain Through Hawaii." *Sunset Magazine* Spring 1917: 7-9, 95-98.

Davids, Hollace and Paul. *The Fires of Pele*. Los Angeles: Pictorial Legends, 1985.

Day, A. Grove. "Hawaii through the Eyes of Mark Twain." *Aloha* Mar.-April 1990: 45-47.

---. Introduction. Mark Twain in Hawaii--*Roughing It In the Sandwich Islands*. By Mark Twain. Honolulu: Mutual Publishing, 1990.

---. Introduction. *Mark Twain's Letters From Hawaii*. By Mark Twain. New York: Appleton-Century, 1966.

Drury, William. "Twain in Hawaii." *Paradise of the Pacific* Jan. 1963: 12.

Emerson, Everett. *The Authentic Mark Twain*. Pennsylvania: U of Pennsylvania P, 1984.

Fatout, Paul. Introduction. *Mark Twain Speaking*. Iowa City: U of Iowa P, 1976.

Ferguson, De Lancey. *Mark Twain, Man and Legend*. New York: Russell and Russell, 1965.

Frear, Walter Francis. *Mark Twain and Hawaii*. Chicago: The Lakeside Press, 1947.

Gerber, John C. *Mark Twain*. Boston: Twayne Publishers, 1988.

Grant, Douglas. *Twain*. London: Oliver and Boyd, 1962.

Hammel, Faye and Sylvan Levey. *Frommer's Hawaii on $45 a Day*. New York: Prentice Hall, 1987.

Horton, Tom. "Mark Twain in the Sandwich Islands." *Honolulu Magazine* Nov. 1979: 88-96.

Howells, William Dean. *My Mark Twain*. New York: Harper and Brothers, 1910.

Independent 17 Aug. 1895: 3.

Jones, William R. Introduction. *Mark Twain in Hawaii*. Golden, Colorado: Outbooks, 1986.

Judd, Gerrit, ed. *A Hawaiian Anthology*. New York: Macmillan, 1967.

Kaplan, Justin. *Mark Twain and His World*. New York: Simon and Schuster, 1974.

Leacock, Stephen. *Mark Twain*. New York: Appleton, 1933.

---. "Letter on Beginning of the Twainian." *The Twainian* June 2, 1941.

Leary, Lewis. *Mark Twain*. Minneapolis: U of Minnesota P, 1968.

Long, E. Hudson and J. R. LeMaster. *The New Mark Twain Handbook*. New York: Garland, 1985.

McClellan, Edwin North. "Mark Twain 'lectured' Hawaii!" *Paradise of the Pacific* Mar. 1936: 9.

Neider, Charles. Introduction. *The Autobiography of Mark Twain*. New York: Harper and Row, 1959.

Pacific Commercial Advertiser 21 Aug. 1895, 1.

Paine, Albert Bigelow. *Mark Twain: A Biography*. 4 vols. New York: Harper & Brothers, 1912.

Pitchford, Genie. "Mark Twain in Hawaii." *Aloha Magazine* Oct. 1961: 35-37.

Rothwell, Mary. "Unawares, A Laughing Angel!" *Paradise of the Pacific* Mar. 1936: 8-10.

Shavelenko, Igor Alexis. *Mark Twain as a Literary Craftsman*. Honolulu: U of Hawaii P, 1945.

Smith, Henry Nash. *Mark Twain, The Development of a Writer*. New York: Atheneum P, 1962.

Stone, Albert E. "Mark Twain and the Story of the Hornet." *The Yale University Library Gazette* 35 (1961): 141-157.

Taylor, Albert P. "How Mark Twain's Newspaper Career Began in the Sandwich Islands." *Paradise of the Pacific* June 1929: 12-15.

Twain, Mark. *The Autobiography of Mark Twain*, ed. Charles Neider. New York: Harper and Row, 1959.

---. *Following the Equator*. Hartford: American Publishing Co., 1897.

---. *Following the Equator*. Hopewell, NJ: Ecco Press, 1992.

---. *Letters From Honolulu Written For the Sacramento Union*, ed. John W. Vandercook. Honolulu: Thomas Nickerson, 1939.

---. [Samuel Langhorne Clemens]. *The Innocents Abroad*. 2 vols. New York: Harper and Brothers, 1911.

---. *The Innocents Abroad* and *Roughing It*, ed. Guy Cardwell. New York: Literary Classics, 1984.

---. *Mark Twain's Letters from Hawaii*, ed. A. Grove Day. New York: Appleton-Century, 1966.

---. *Mark Twain in Hawaii*, ed. William R. Jones. Golden, Colorado: Outbooks, 1986.

---. *Mark Twain in Hawaii--Roughing It In the Sandwich Islands*, ed. A. Grove Day. Honolulu: Mutual Publishing, 1990.

---. *Mark Twain Speaking*, ed. Paul Fatout. Iowa City: U of Iowa P, 1976.

---. "My Platonic Sweetheart." *Harpers* Dec. 1912.

---. *Roughing It*. New York: Harper and Brothers, 1959.

---. *Roughing It, Volume I*. New York: Harper and Row, 1871.

---. *The Portable Mark Twain*, ed. Bernard DeVoto. New York: Viking Press, 1963.

---. *The Unabridged Mark Twain*, ed. Lawrence Teacher. Philadelphia: Running Press, 1976.

---. *Volume I-Letters From the Sandwich Islands*, ed. Joan Abramson. Norfork, Australia: Island Heritage Ltd., 1975.

Vandercook, John W. Introduction. *Letters from Honolulu Written for the Sacramento Union*. By Mark Twain. Honolulu: Thomas Nickerson, 1939.

West, Gary V. "The Development of the Mark Twain Persona in the Early Travel Letters." *Mark Twain Journal* 3 (1980): 13-16.

Wilson, Willard. *Mark Twain Returns to Hawaii*. Honolulu: U of Hawaii P, 1969.

Zmijewski, David. "Hawaii Waits a Legend." *Mark Twain Journal* 26 (1988): 21-26.